Sometimes

They Were Mountains

By Bradley Pinch

ISBN (Hardcover): 978-0-6487127-2-5
ISBN (e-Book): 978-0-6487127-3-2

BLANK
EXPECTATIONS

A catalogue record for this work is available from the National Library of Australia

I would like to dedicate this book to all those who have suffered, all those that have made brave decisions and all of those who have embraced a world that at times tests their entire living being.

This book is dedicated to the human within all of us.

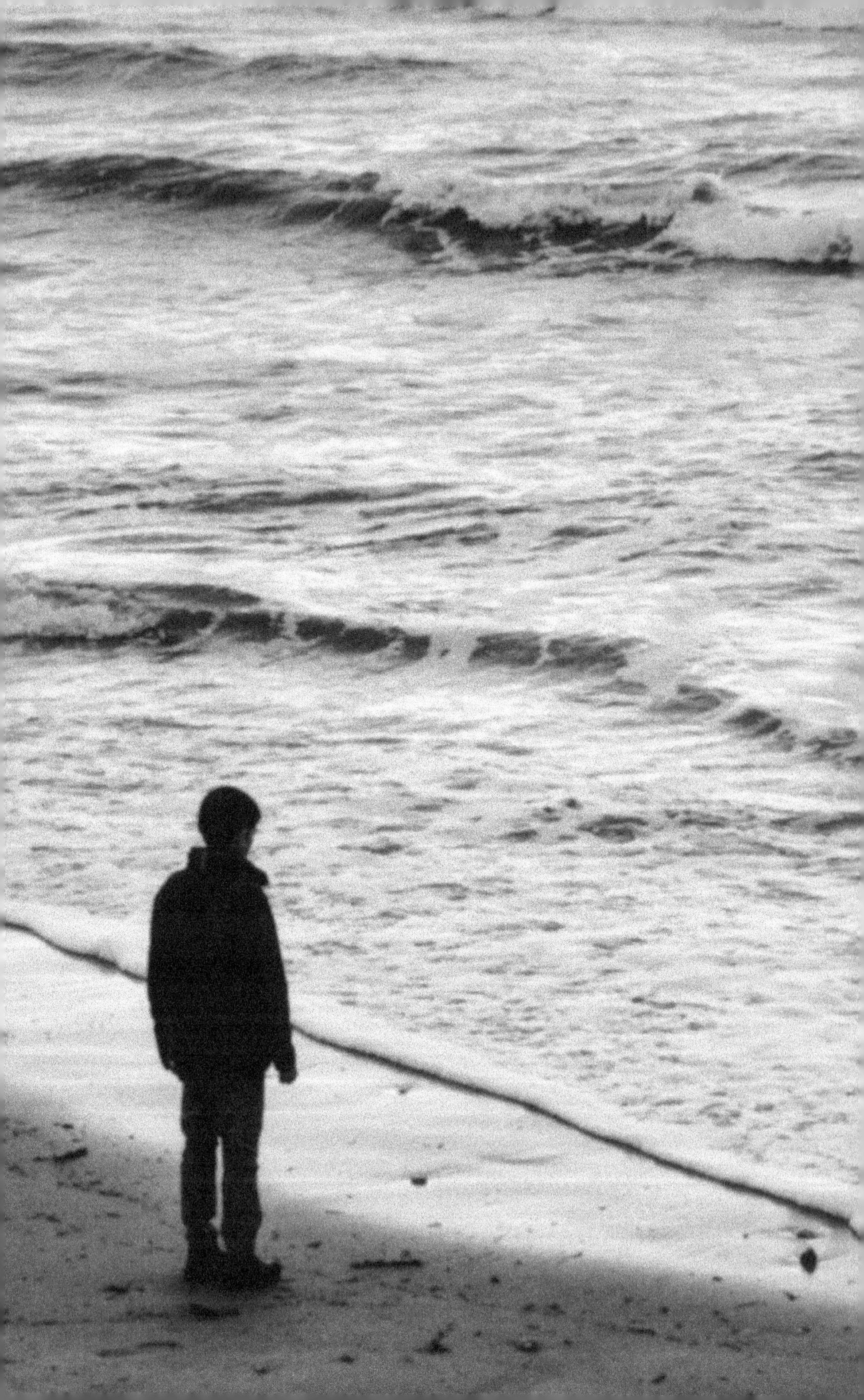

At last I wake to the sound
of birds
Finally I hear them

As though I have always heard them
That sound
It makes me smile

And I sit
I sit for awhile
Silent eyes look to the sky and see

A reflection of what I can be
To be

I know
I will

and the world will continue
Still.

Words used to drop into my head like that
They're starting to come back

To open the mind
and the heart sit still
At peace I will continue to feel.

-- The calm before the storm

To the log that was once a tree
You will again arise to walk and breathe
I thank the gift that has crossed my path
And long for the day we are not apart.
I was once a tree too

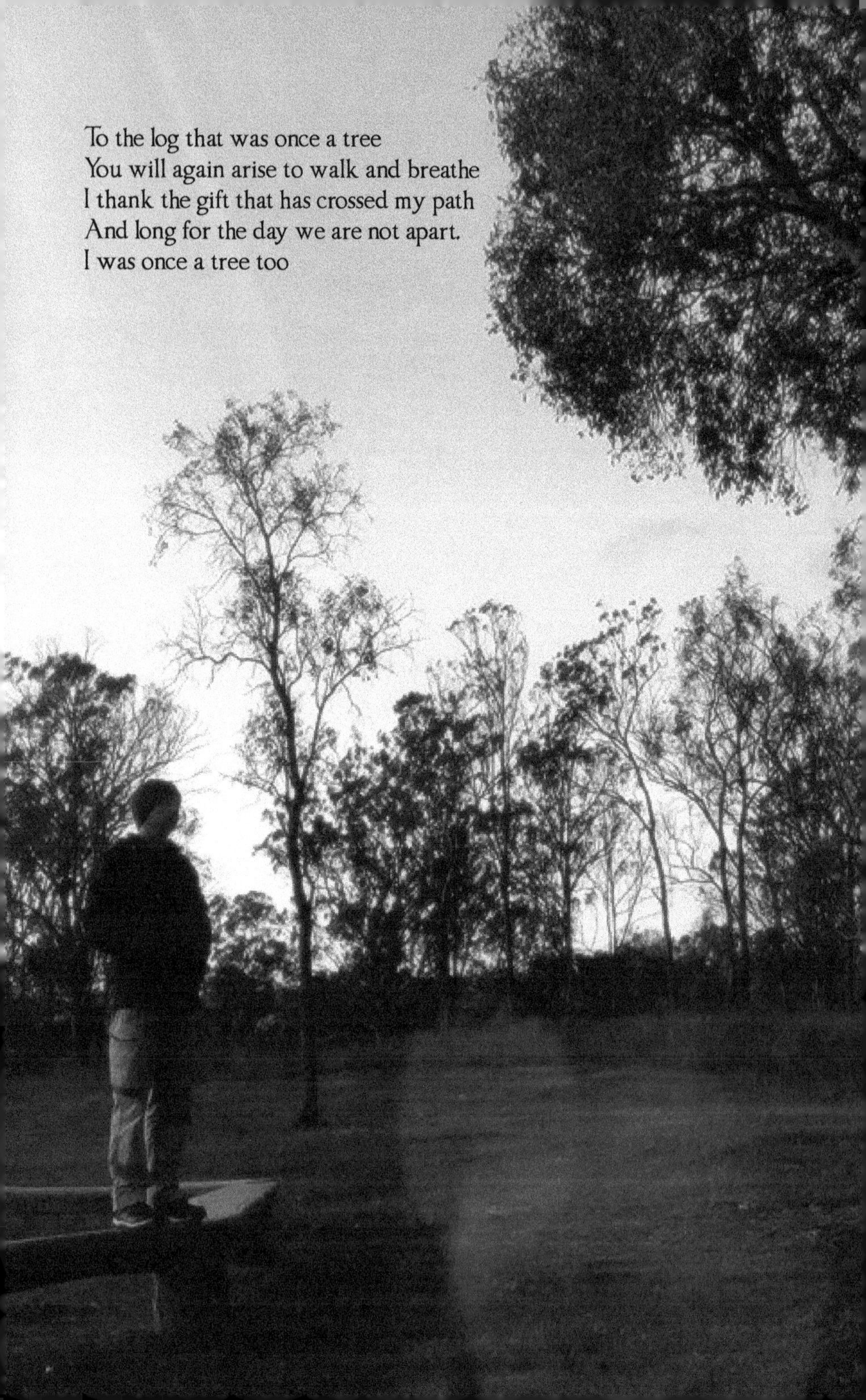

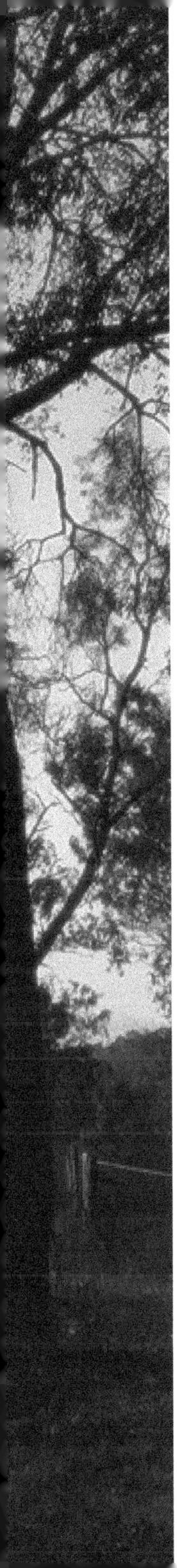

Tears in my eyes
Actual tears
In my eyes
As I now know I'm alive
Alive to walk
To be free
To rediscover me
Me for what I am
Me for all I am
Staring into the abyss
I think of what I have missed
The boy inside smiles

What's that sound I hear and fear?
When my life's journey is not so clear
Clear to see and be
Not to hide from Life's tree
The branches grow into the sky
If only I could touch the top and feel alive
What fear buries me today?
For that I cannot say
But to face it and embrace the journey of life
Will be forever the fright of life.

-- A confession

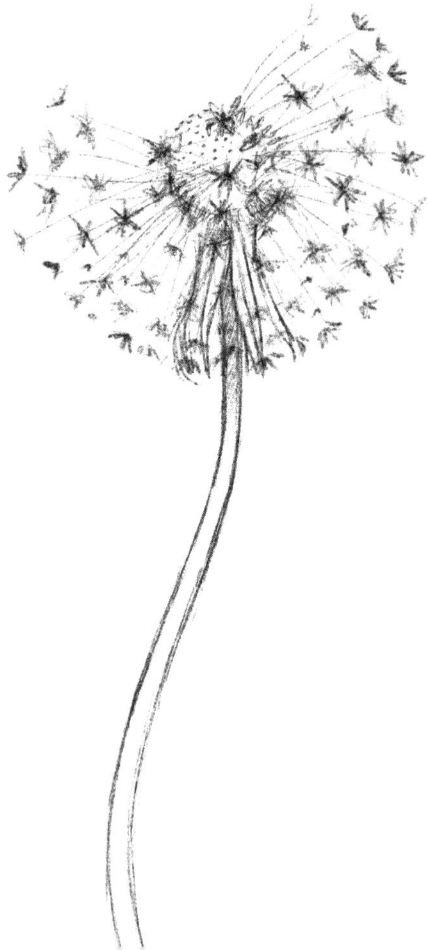

But what is fate and life in which we breathe
To a love that hopefully we will never leave.

-- Wanting

Don't forget about me.

Please.

Get off the floor
Don't judge yourself
Against these lies

This hollowness has come
To rise from the smoke
and strangle your passionate zest.

To walk with your own reflection
Is the true test
Of this path I have found

This caring is new
To forgive yourself can be hard to do
My reality ...

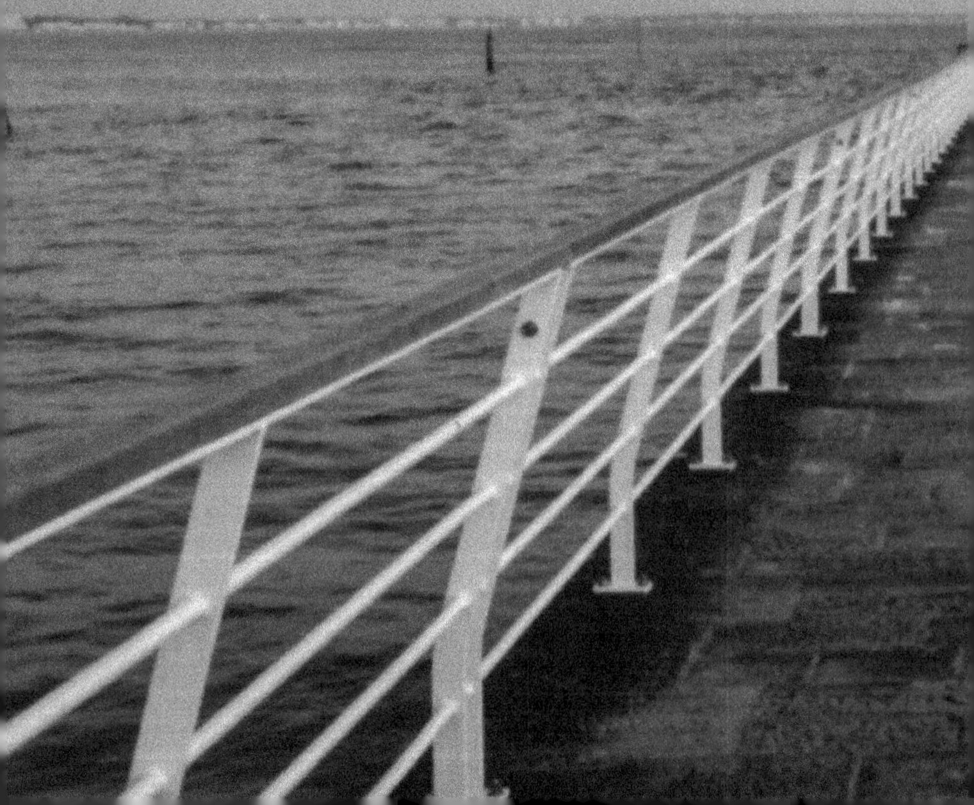

... My perspective cut down in streams
What have I done?

The darkness of night
Cutting through my character
Tasting the bitterness from your knife

I felt all of the spite
Why?
Why do you orchestrate attacks on my life?

—When did I become your enemy

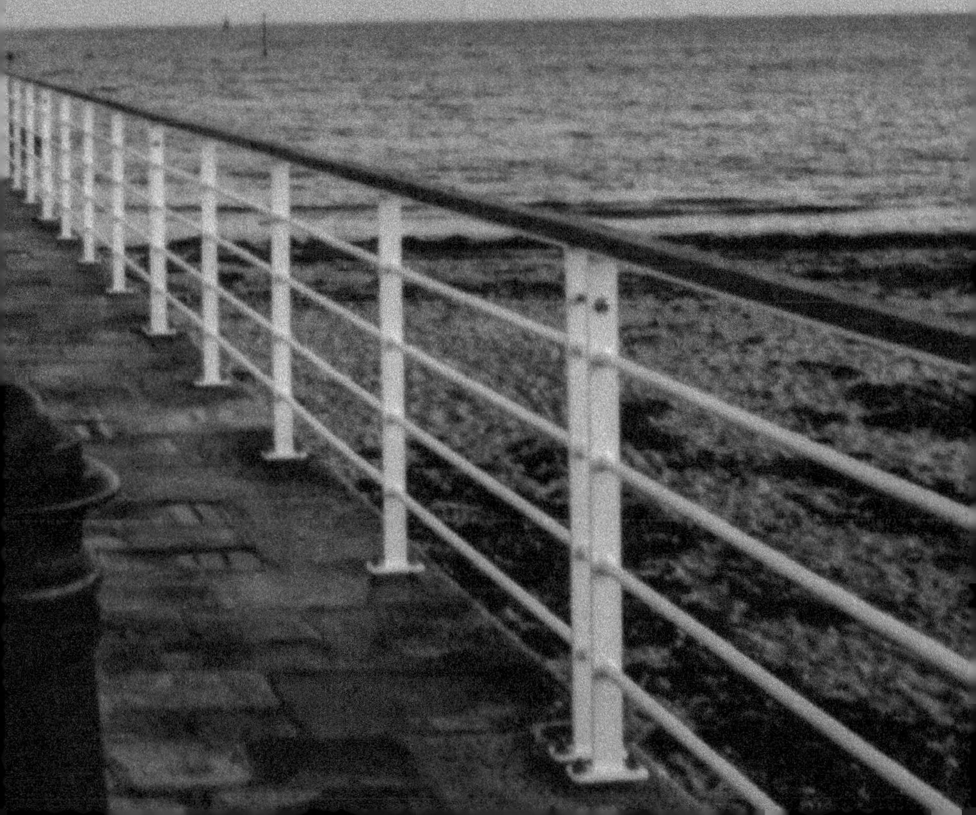

To have a game played with your life
To have your core cut with a butter knife

--The mouse to the cat

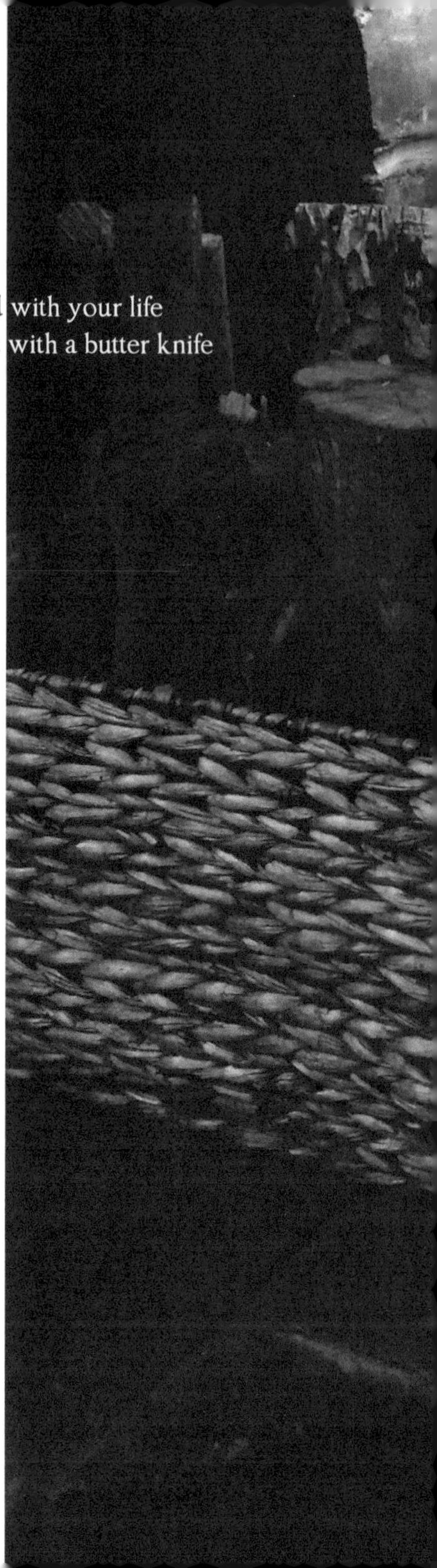

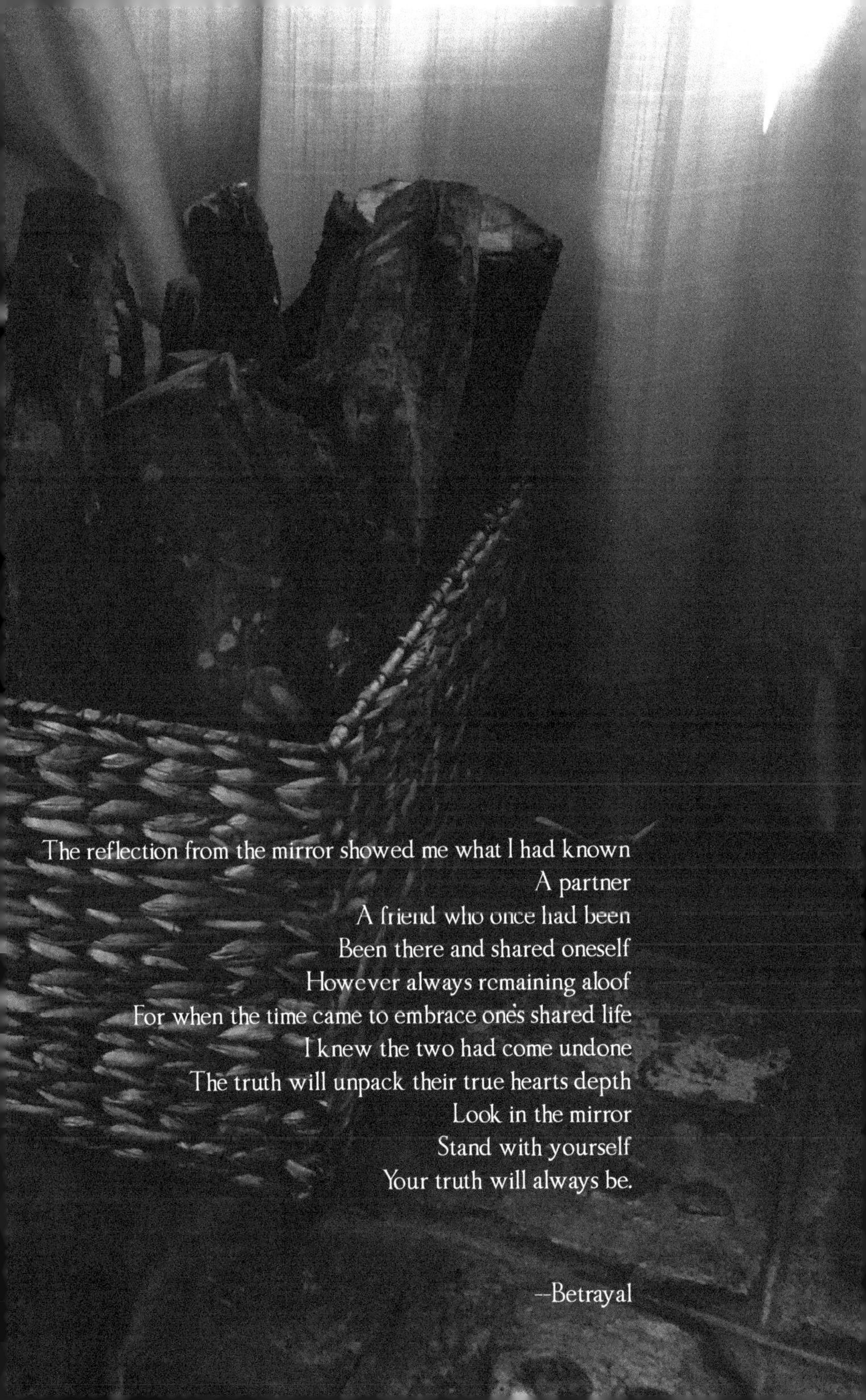

The reflection from the mirror showed me what I had known
A partner
A friend who once had been
Been there and shared oneself
However always remaining aloof
For when the time came to embrace one's shared life
I knew the two had come undone
The truth will unpack their true hearts depth
Look in the mirror
Stand with yourself
Your truth will always be.

—Betrayal

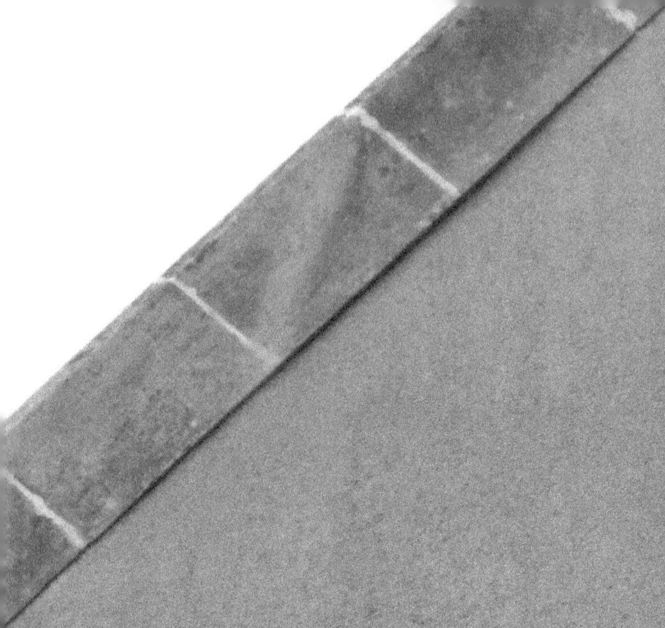

A twisted mind

that alters self-control

Bears a hefty tax

Will you pay with my life

—Unveiled

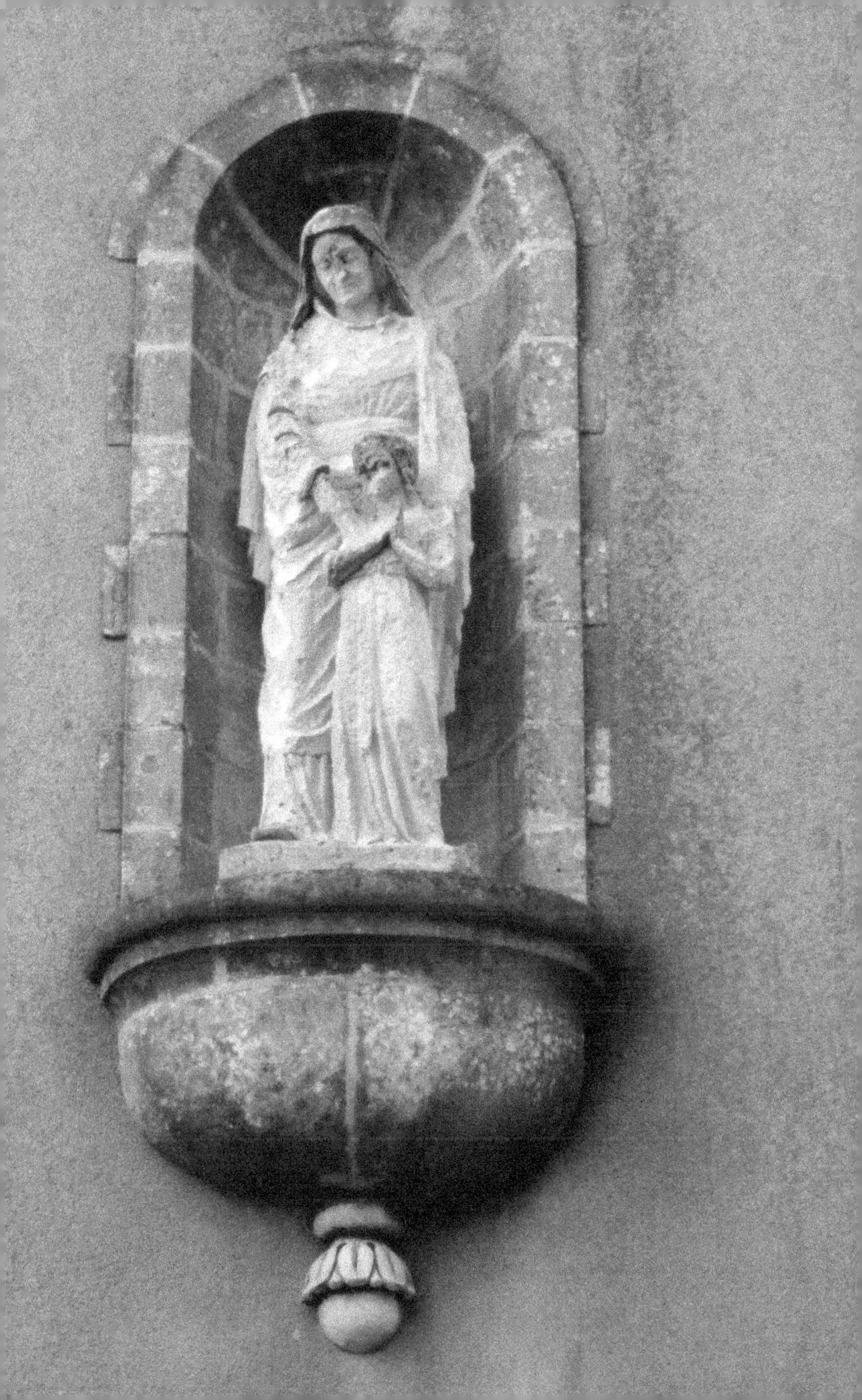

I am so tired

All the time

Wondering

My world has fallen apart

When did I lose myself?
Was it when we became a family?
No, they enhanced me

When did I lose myself?
Was it when I gave you all of me?

When I could no longer recognise
My portrait shaped in sunsets
And sandcastles?

My DNA has been altered
I am nowhere to be found

-- Missing

To be inspired by behaviour
Feel one with your neighbour
To crash down to the depths of hell
To sit all alone with no one to tell
To loom into one's mirror
To only see one's face
To walk down the corridor
To sit alone on the floor
To dig deep within
To feel every moment is a sin
Alone

-- There is no throne

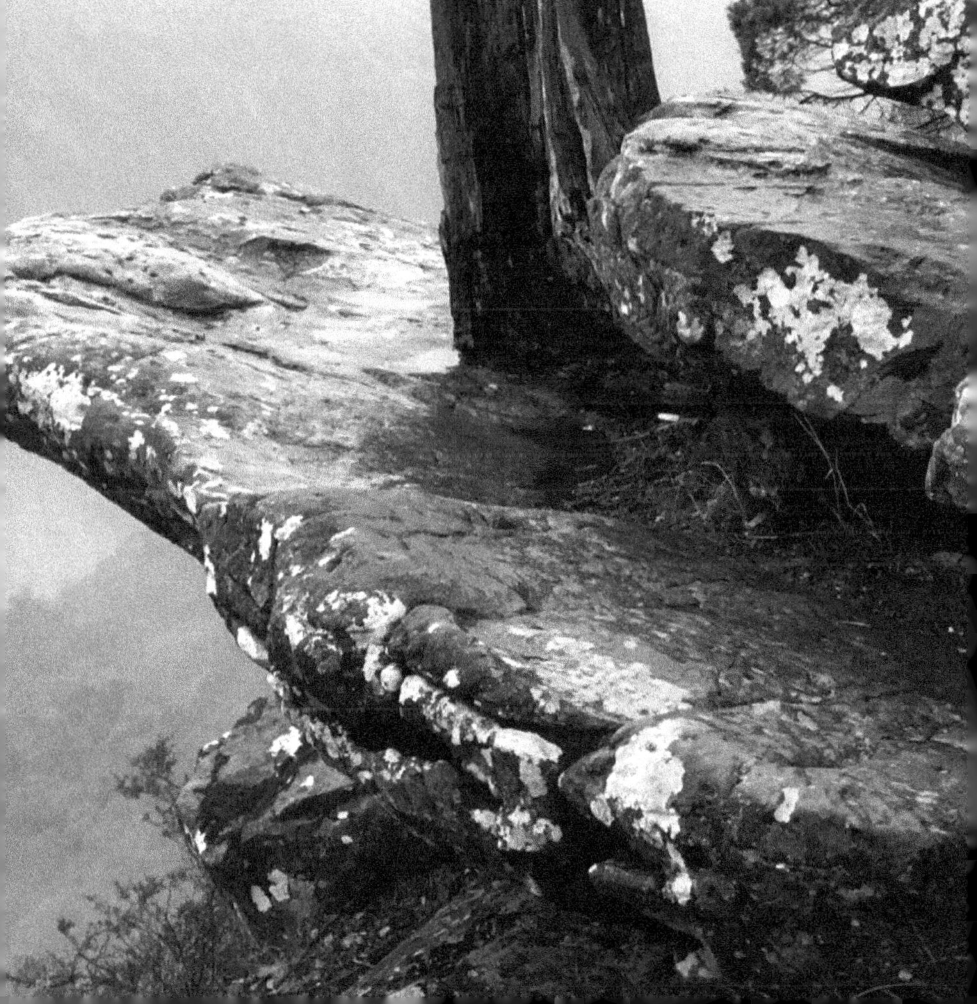

When I see my heart is free, I will meet my true reflection.

-- An oath

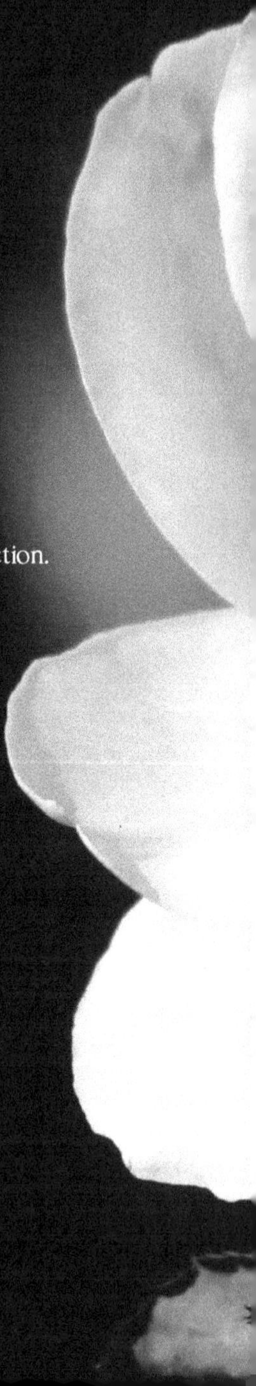

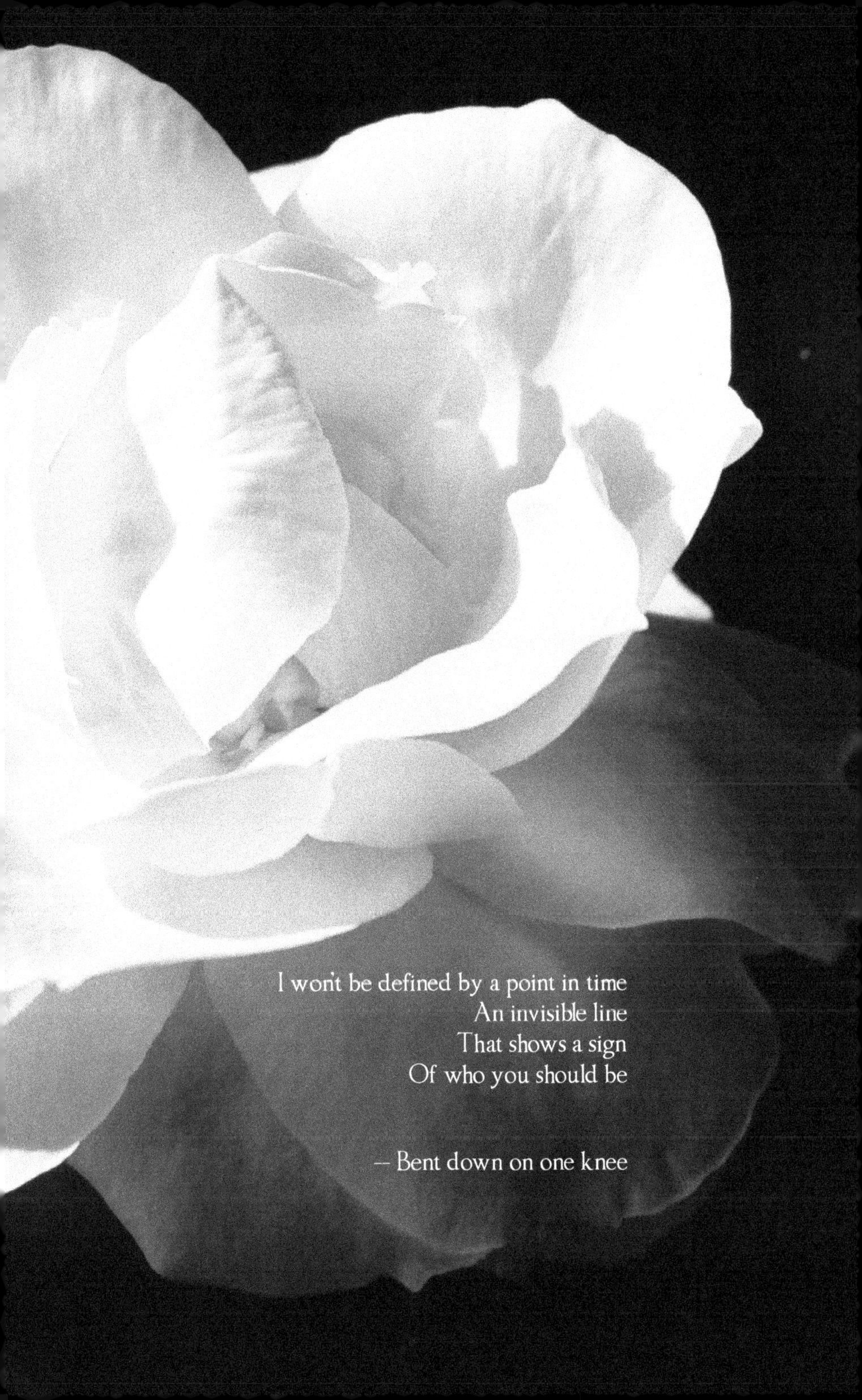

I won't be defined by a point in time
An invisible line
That shows a sign
Of who you should be

– Bent down on one knee

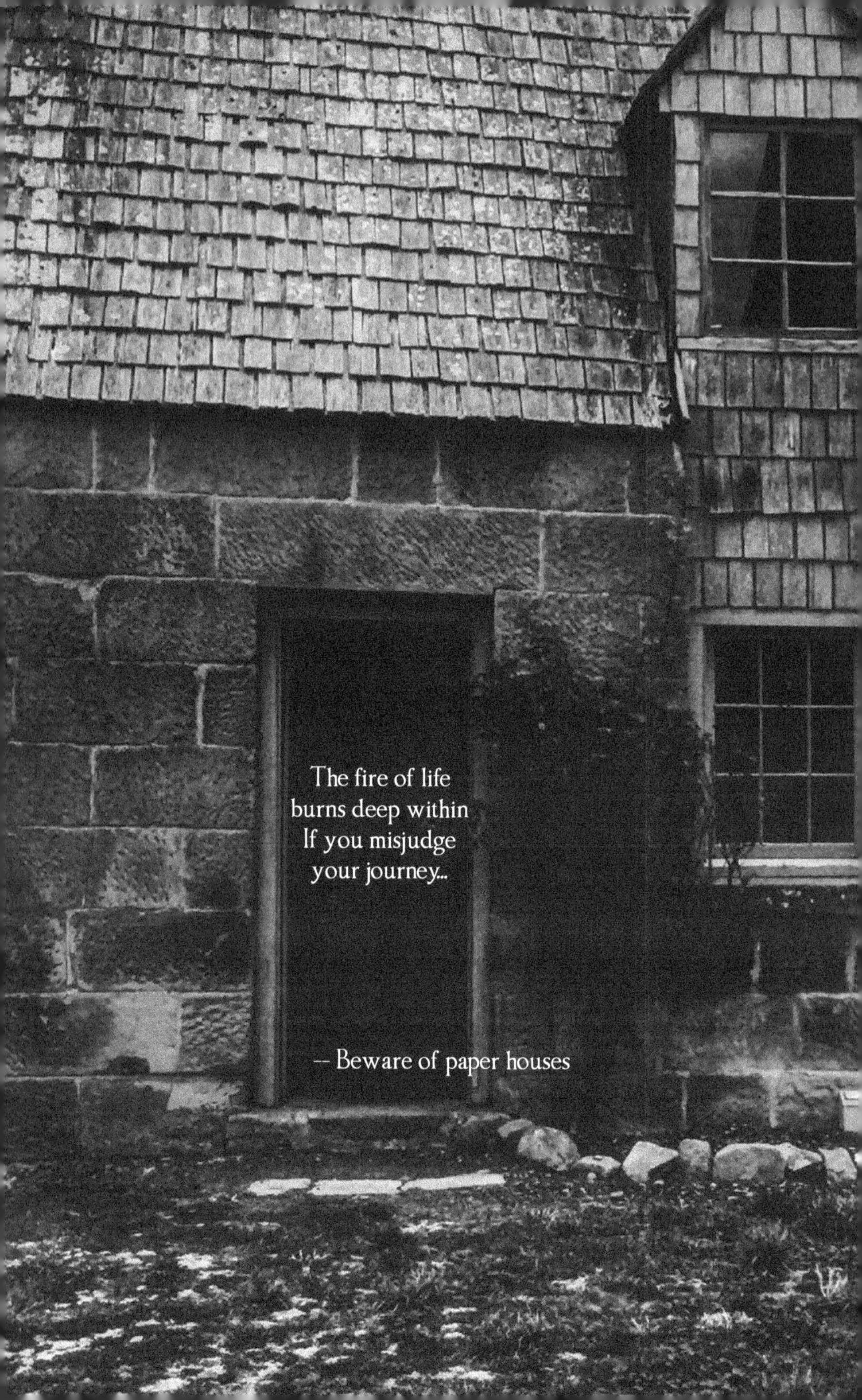

The fire of life
burns deep within
If you misjudge
your journey...

-- Beware of paper houses

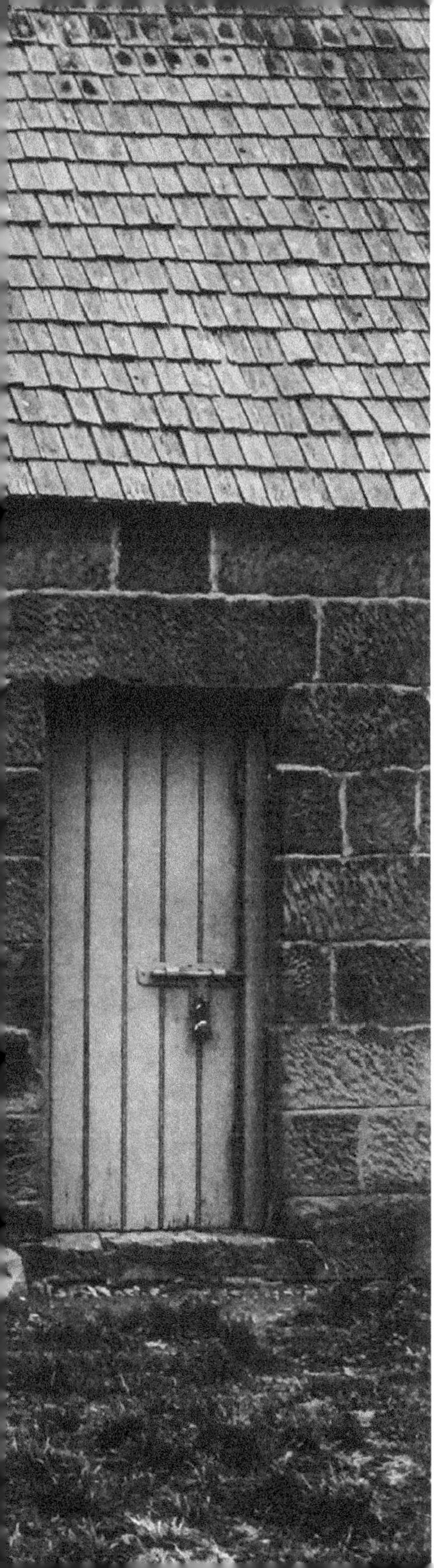

I walk to the door
and entered what was once my home
I walked into a total unknown
I could but only see a small part of me

What is a home?
What should I see?
Mine, a dying part of me

The walls once stood strong
and the roof was proud

-- (For) A Stranger in my own home

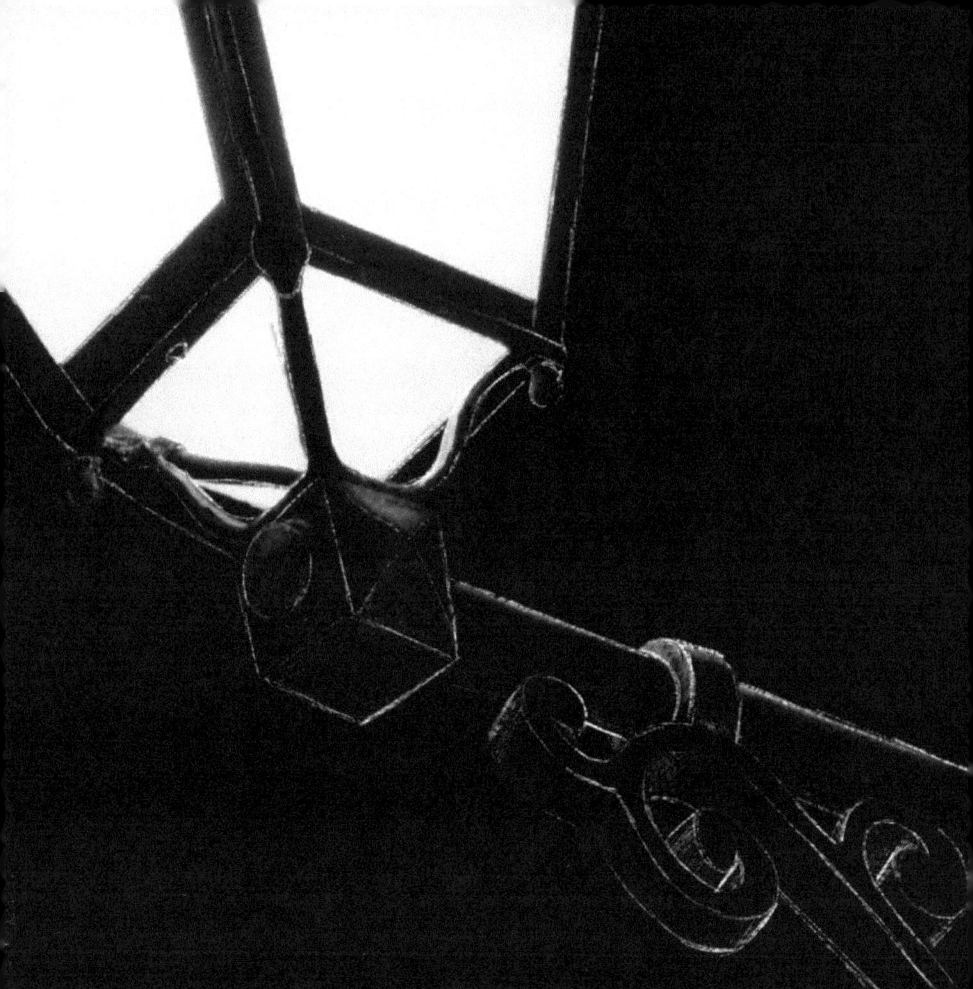

I run down the distant road
It is really hard to see
Trying to realise my mind's load
Where, when and how I'll be

Playing the music that ignites thought
To build one's resilience is truly the key
Facing the decisions I've made and what they have taught
To allow all of yourself to be

I know what happened

I was there

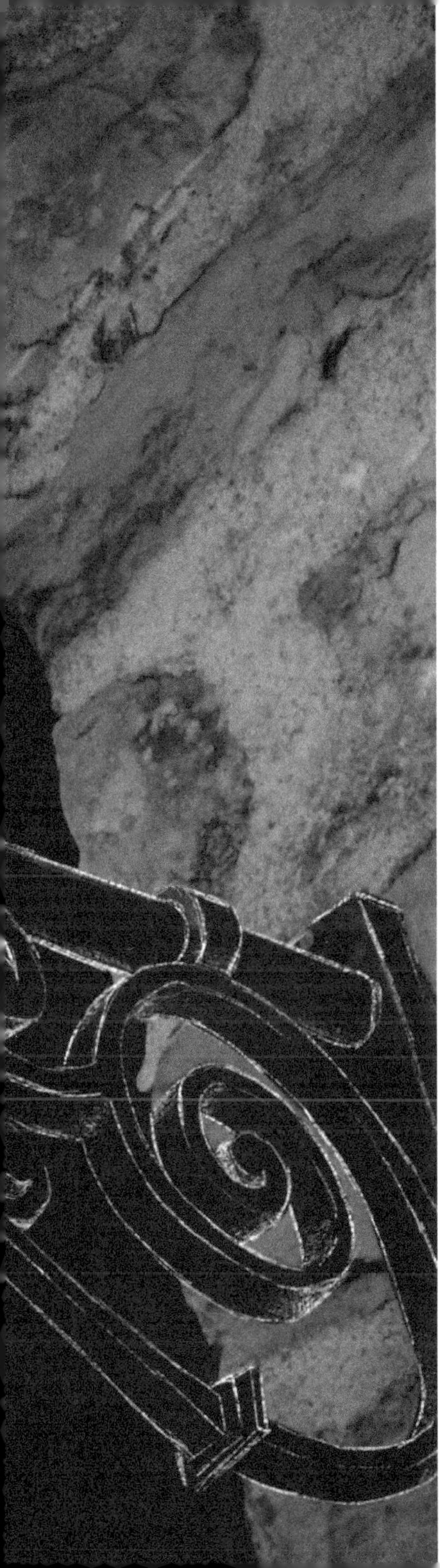

To have your heart taken apart
To not know the moving parts

I'm no surgeon

I can almost feel every second tick by
And stop as I try
The heightened awareness over me

Like a child that needs to burn their energy
For that right now
is me

As I exhaust my body
to free my mind
I hope that it will be kind

Just let me sit and be
Let my dreams sit alone on the shelf
With myself

-- Facing the mirror

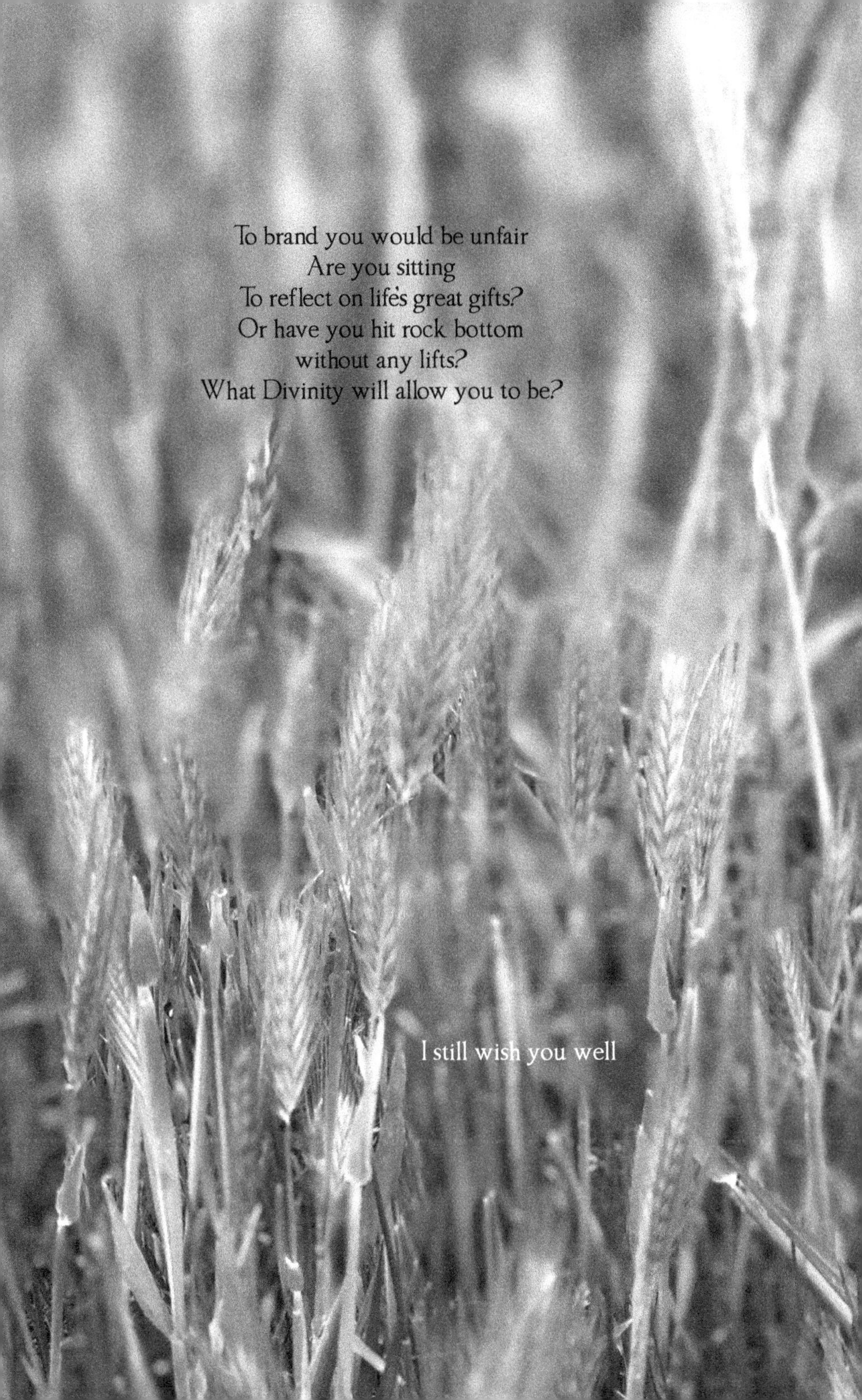

To brand you would be unfair
Are you sitting
To reflect on life's great gifts?
Or have you hit rock bottom
without any lifts?
What Divinity will allow you to be?

I still wish you well

Words can set a scene
be what your mind has seen

Words are your spoken voice
Not as streamlined as a Rolls Royce

Words can be your internal arrow
Fired direct and narrow

Your words have weight on those you care
Of your words beware

To forgive is not to forget

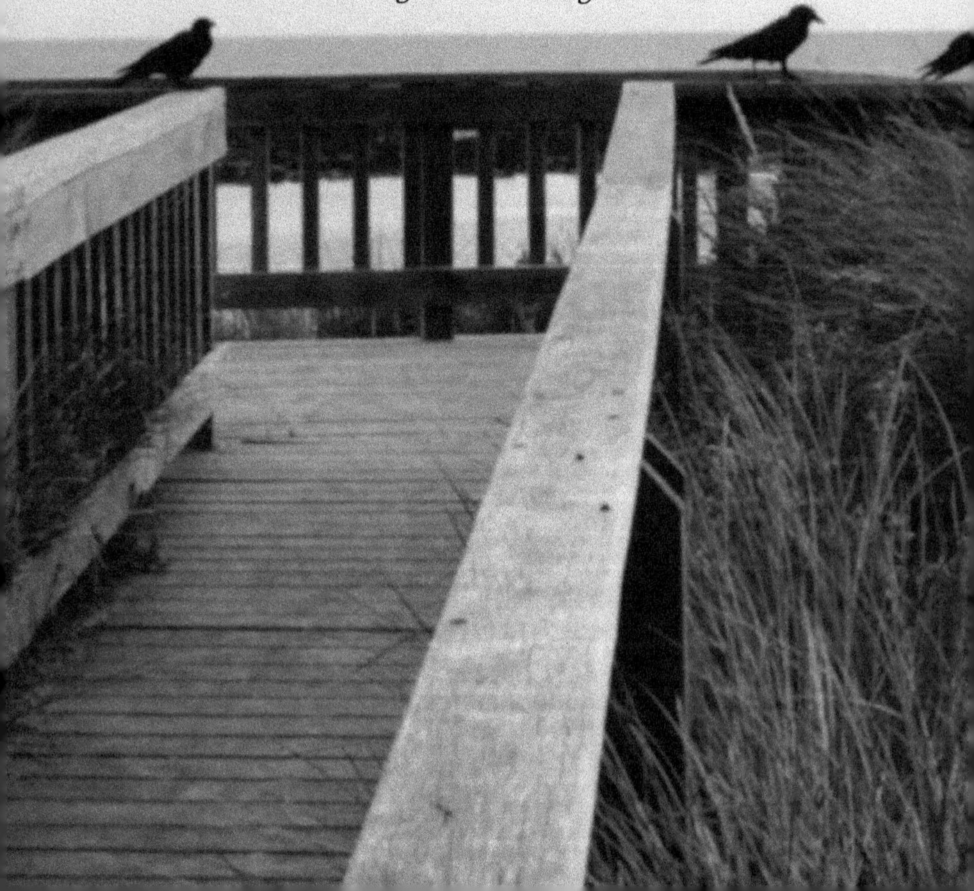

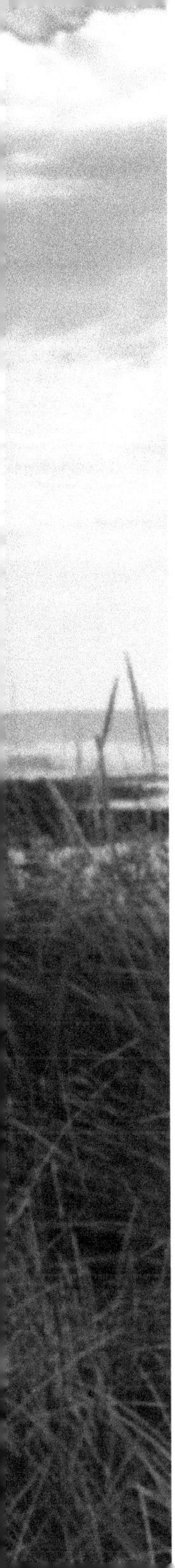

Embrace what is out there
For you do not know
There could be seeds
Dropped for you to grow
Open the curtains
You can see.
If I can get up
Look up to the sky
All of my senses will know

-- I am alive

People's lives have them arrive in strange places
Assuming they have the answer to all the faces

Present me to a judge

From where is that your judgement comes
What has made you equate to your total sum

Narrow your thoughts

I try to remove the cancer of judgements

Your mirror's words are not my own

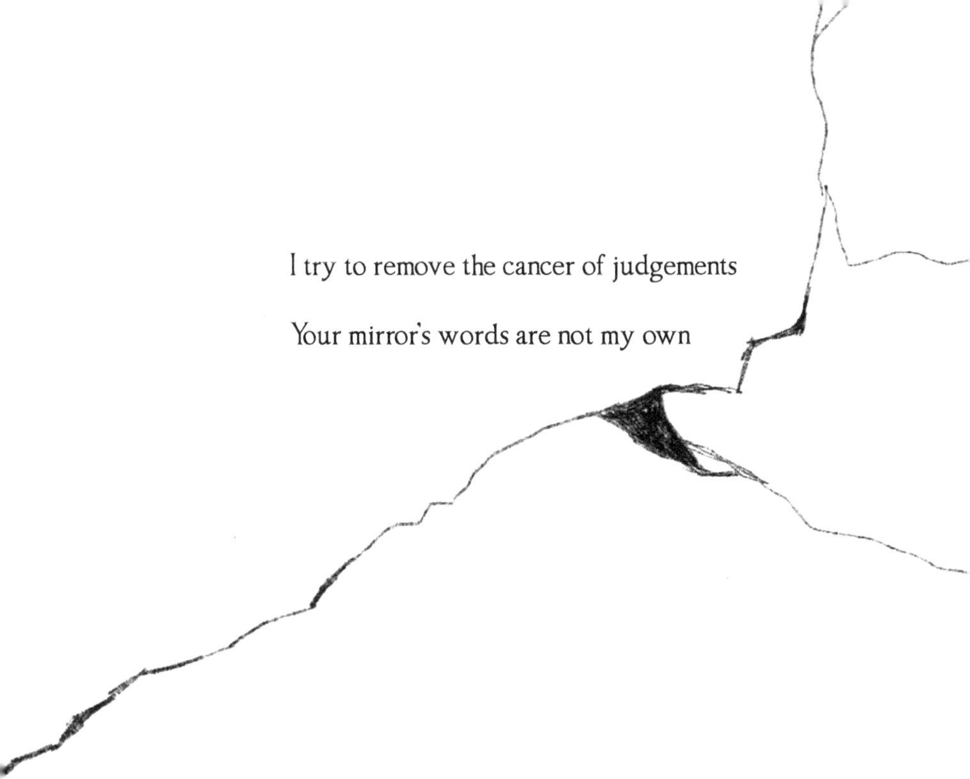

It is not me I see
When I walk in the carpark at night
It is there where I see lonely sights
When I sit alone
When I walk along the street
Is this a state of mind?
When you venture into your darkest internal fight
It is here where you need to dance within life's light
For if you always see lonely sights
So awake and embrace all that is near
And walk into the corridor of fear

-- Learning to walk alone

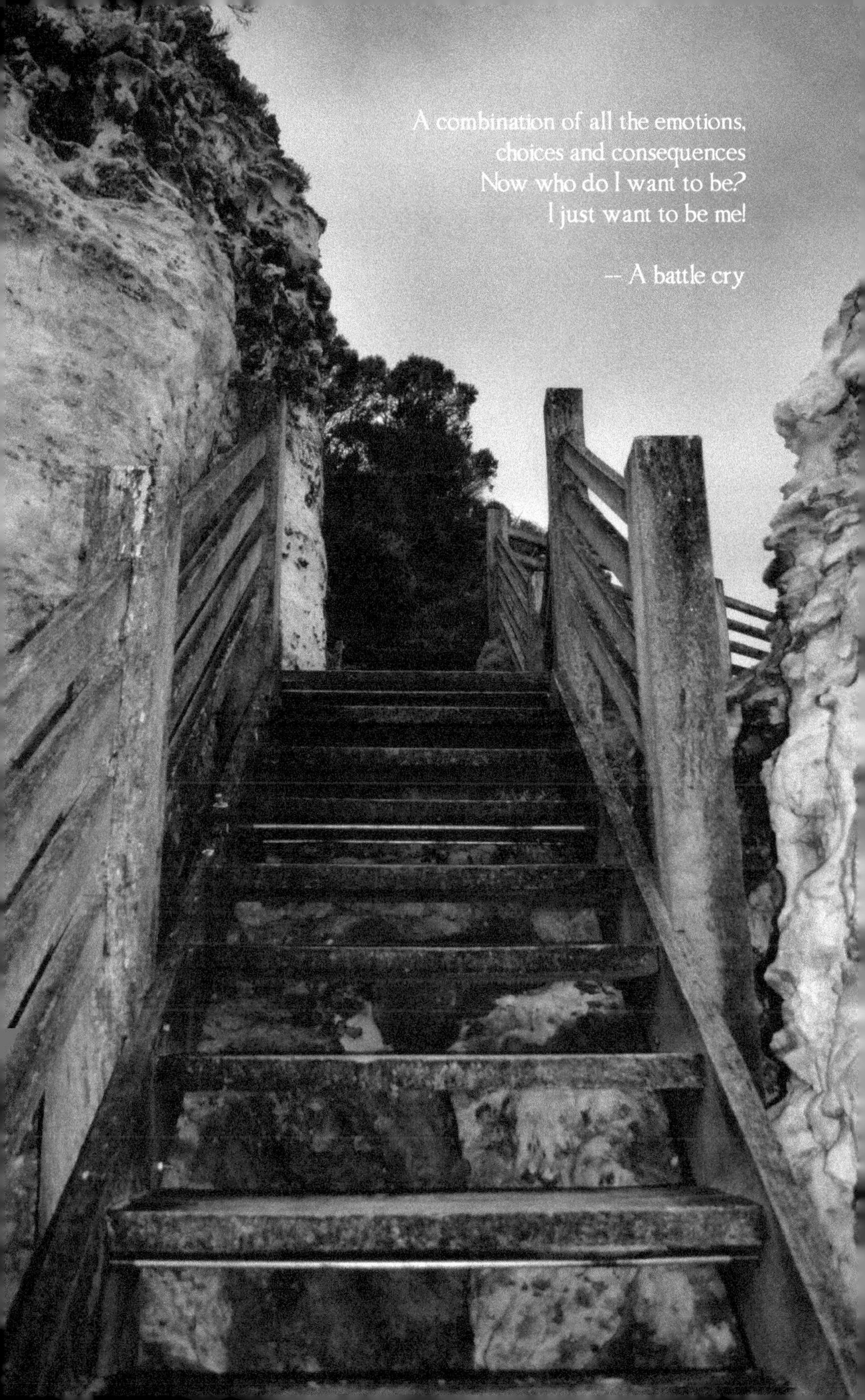
A combination of all the emotions,
choices and consequences
Now who do I want to be?
I just want to be me!

-- A battle cry

You will never be able to sleep
When your well of loneliness is this deep
in these uncertain times
Read between the lines
For you are strong, kind
The stork of life delivered nutrients from its beak
Arise and walk where you once would run
For you are starving to have fun
No more lonely sights you see
It is time to let your mind be free.

-- I am not weak

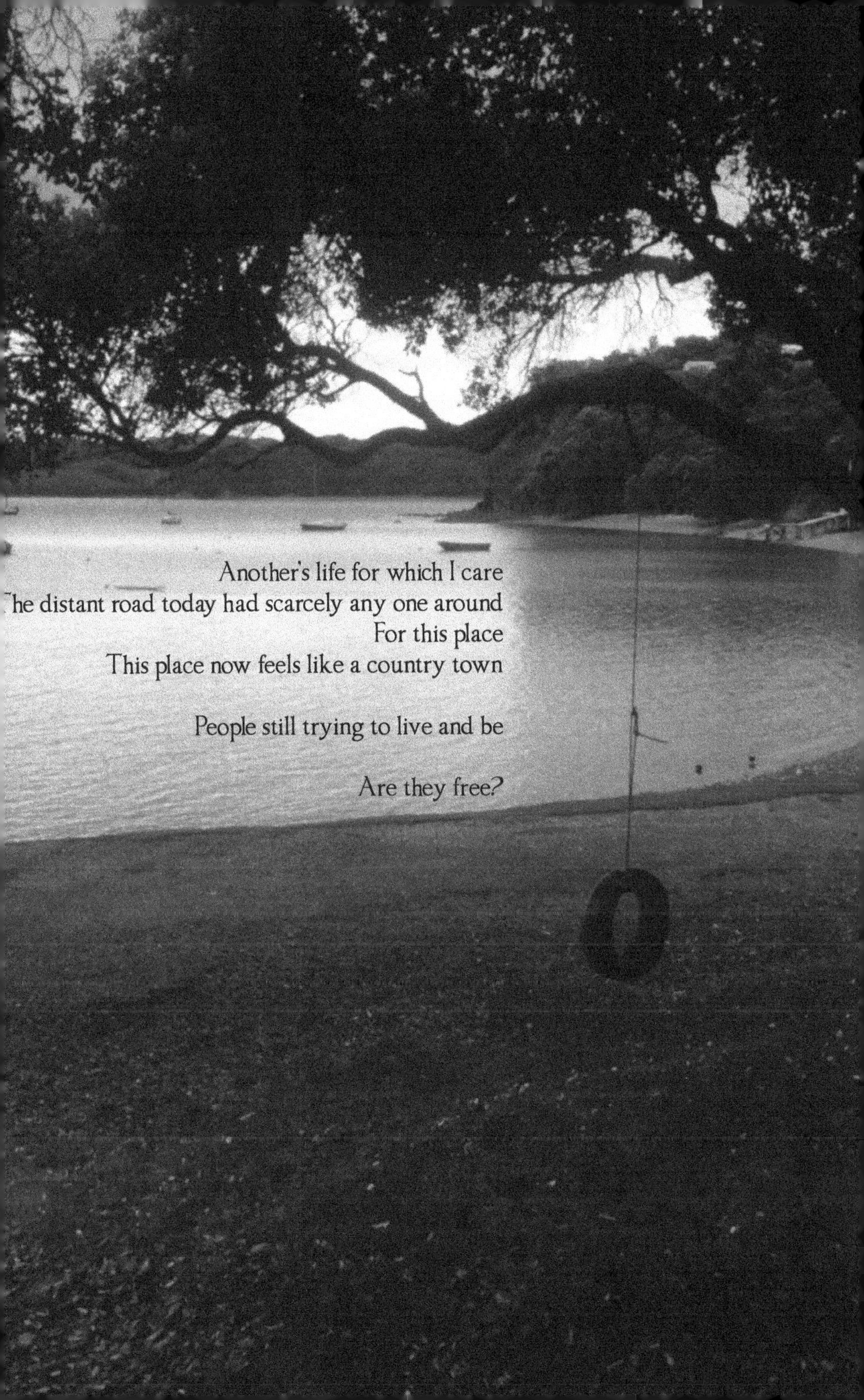

Another's life for which I care
The distant road today had scarcely any one around
For this place
This place now feels like a country town

People still trying to live and be

Are they free?

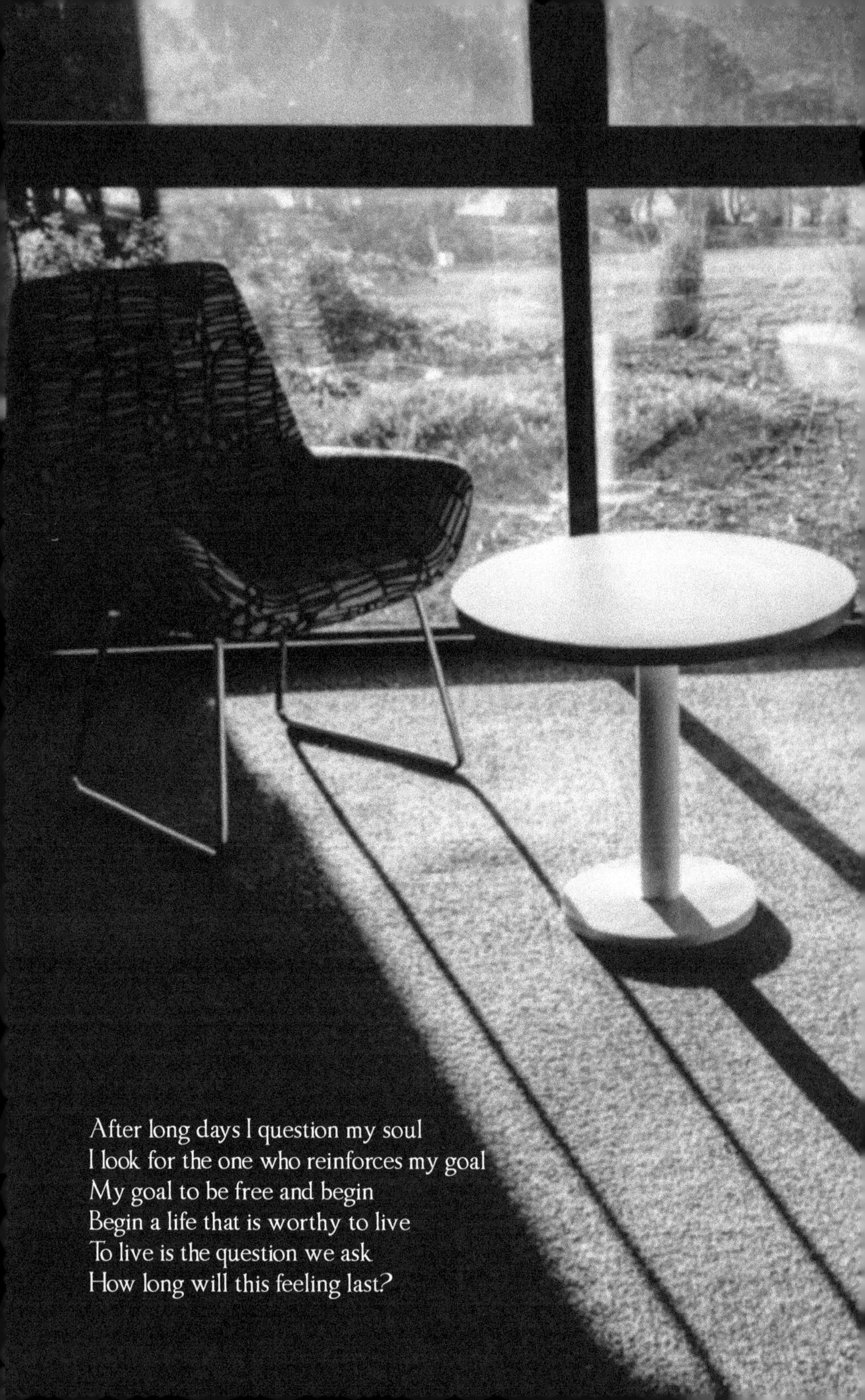

After long days I question my soul
I look for the one who reinforces my goal
My goal to be free and begin
Begin a life that is worthy to live
To live is the question we ask
How long will this feeling last?

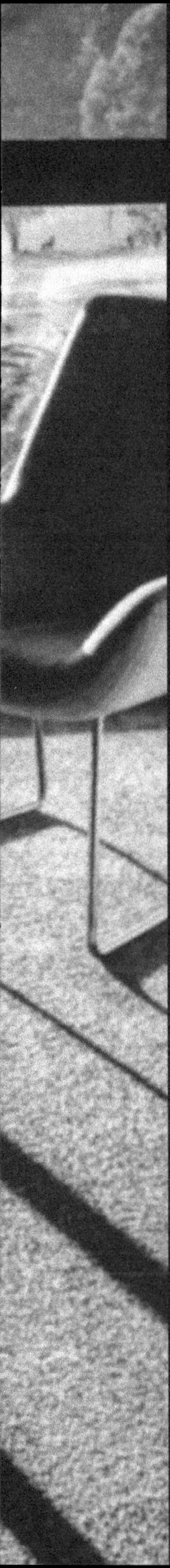

Have you ever heard the roots of the Norfolk Pines moan?
Or have you looked at the sea
As it returns from land completely free

What about a bee that lands on a flower
You haven't noticed it was circling for an hour
Alone, alone with your thoughts

Alone with all you have been taught
Have ever notice a swallow who protects their young
For right then they acknowledge life's sum

What about the dog that stares into the distance
Utilising all that's been given without resistance
Now I see you all alone on that chair

-- Alone

Sleep
Now or forever
Sleep
Some would say never
For the path that is chosen will be
I welcome the vision I see.

Sleep

The feeling that makes us one at heart
A heart that beats long and last
In a world that doesn't care
To build one we will always share
Share the feelings that make this great
The feelings that will one day seal our fate

Insomnia

Time is ultimately never defined
Go mingle as the roulettes spin

— Blurred reality begins.

I can't see my reflection

— An Epiphany

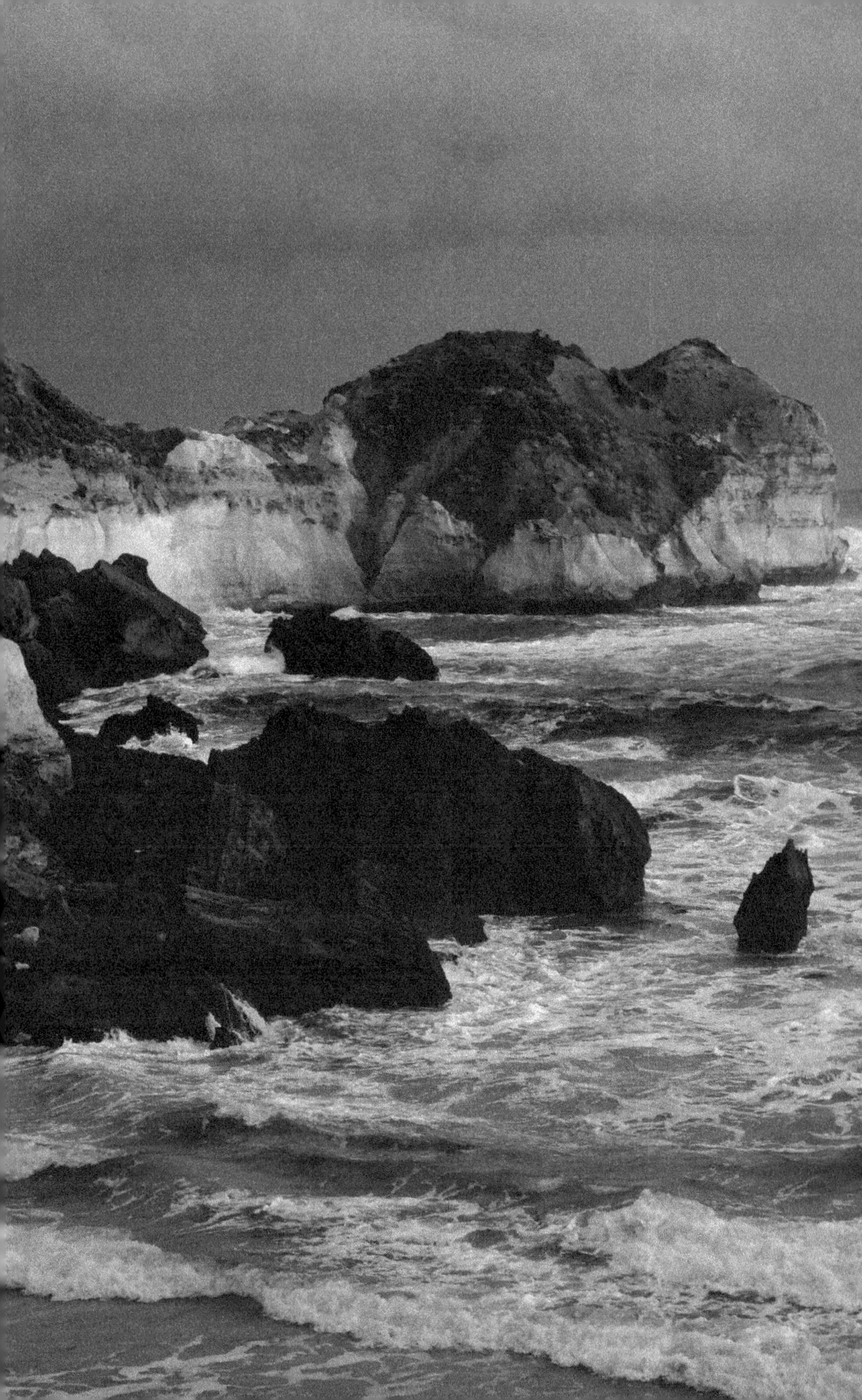

My heart was taken by the light
Impacting my overall sight
My vision had been severely blurred
My mind presented of only what it heard
For now my heart feels true
Each day brings it something new
It ponders the feelings deep inside
Now very grateful of its emotional tide
For my heart it is clear and it is true
It is now beating in time for only the sacred few.

-- The sound of drums

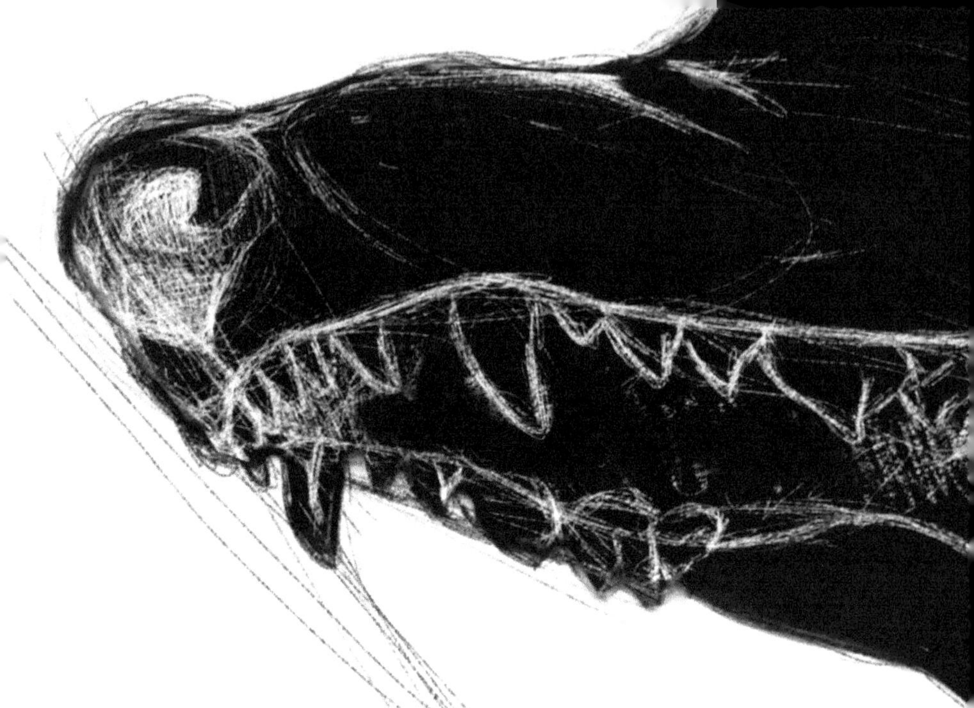

To then subside within
Showing that blurred reality is thin
I embrace the darkness, mist and fog
With the deafening growl of the devil's dogs

-- Hunted

The beast in me
Yearns to be part of a community
Where has that community been?
What have the eyes of the world seen?
Do they see all it can be?
Or are they selfish just like me

-- Inside the black dog

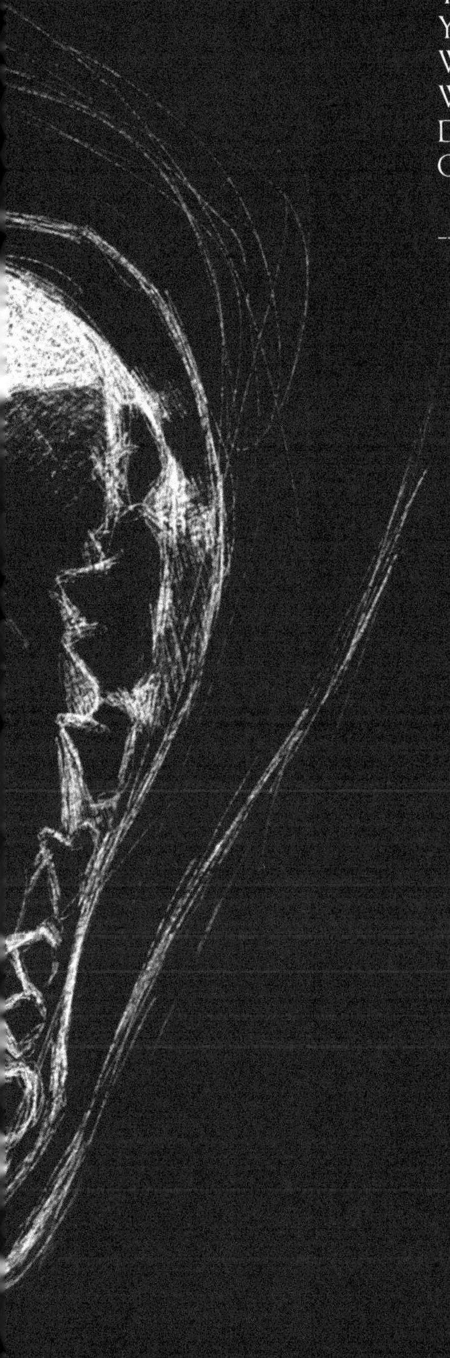

The sky so blue up high
This feeling of being alive
The water running to the sea
Now my eyes can see

-- The Blueprint

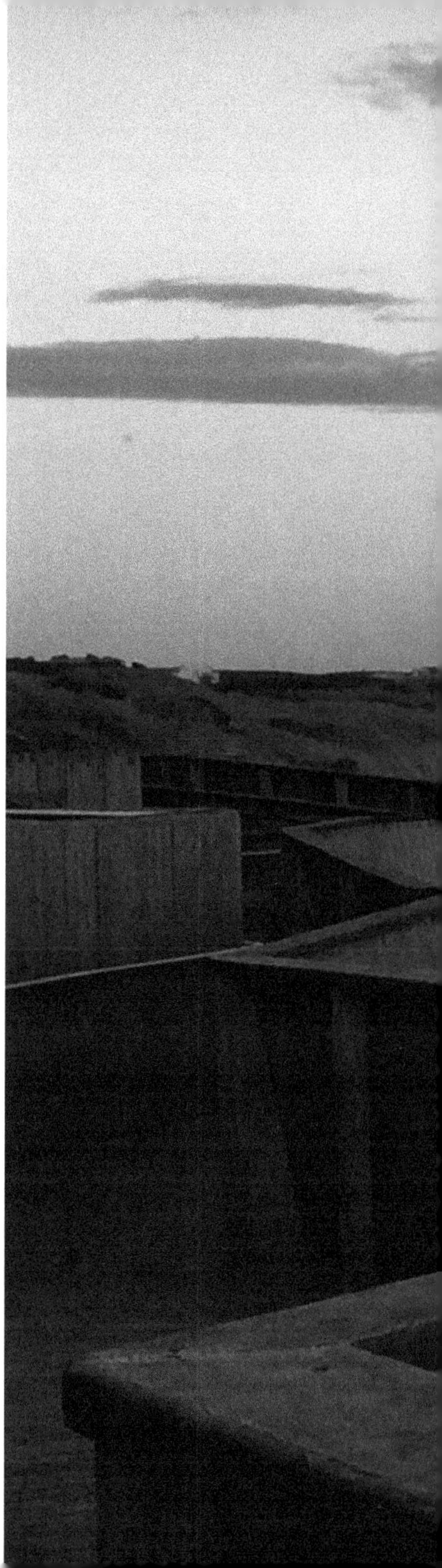

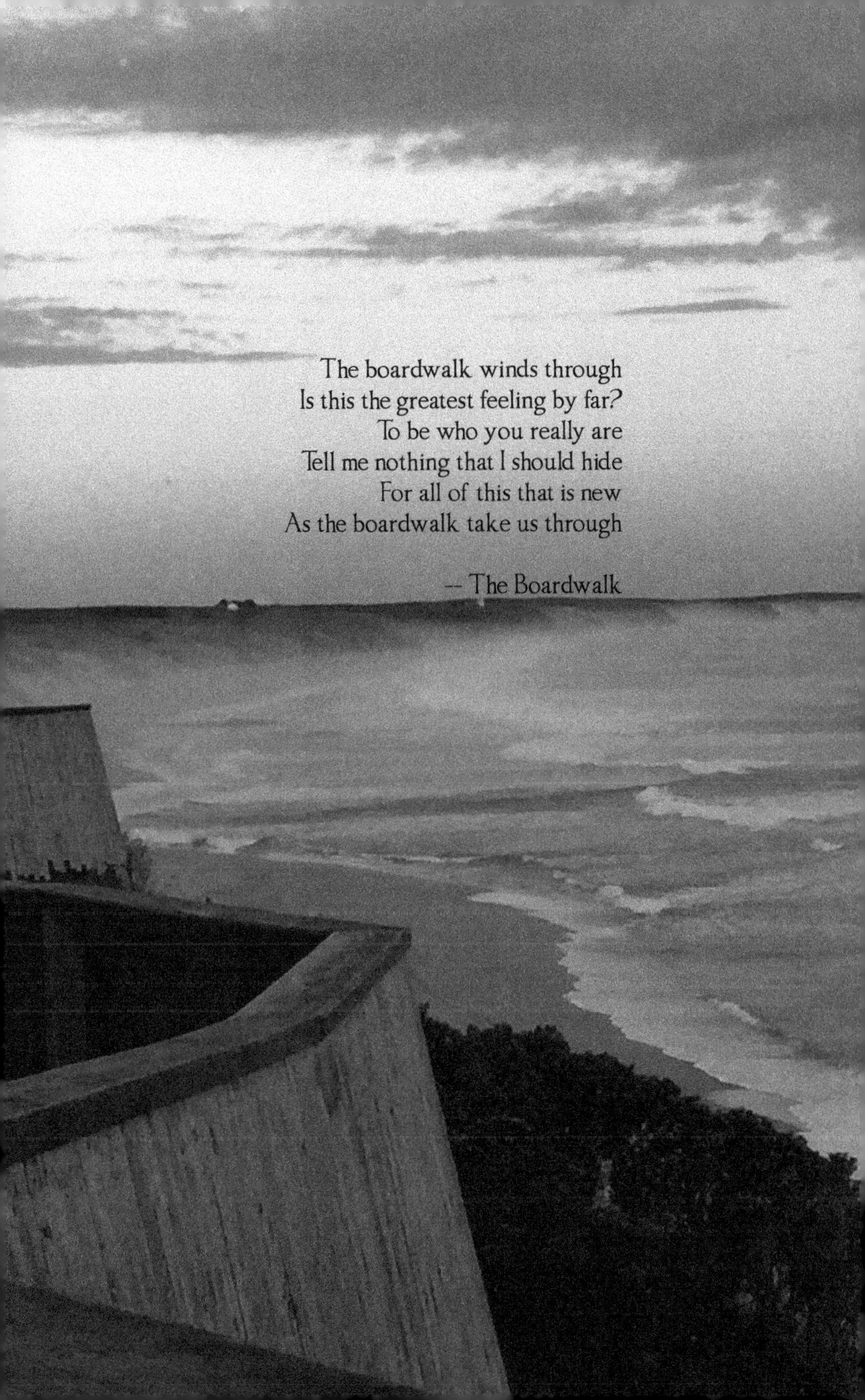

The boardwalk winds through
Is this the greatest feeling by far?
To be who you really are
Tell me nothing that I should hide
For all of this that is new
As the boardwalk take us through

-- The Boardwalk

Feeling the embrace of the sun
The depth of reality equalling the sum
The path floods
With the tide
Why does it make me feel alive?

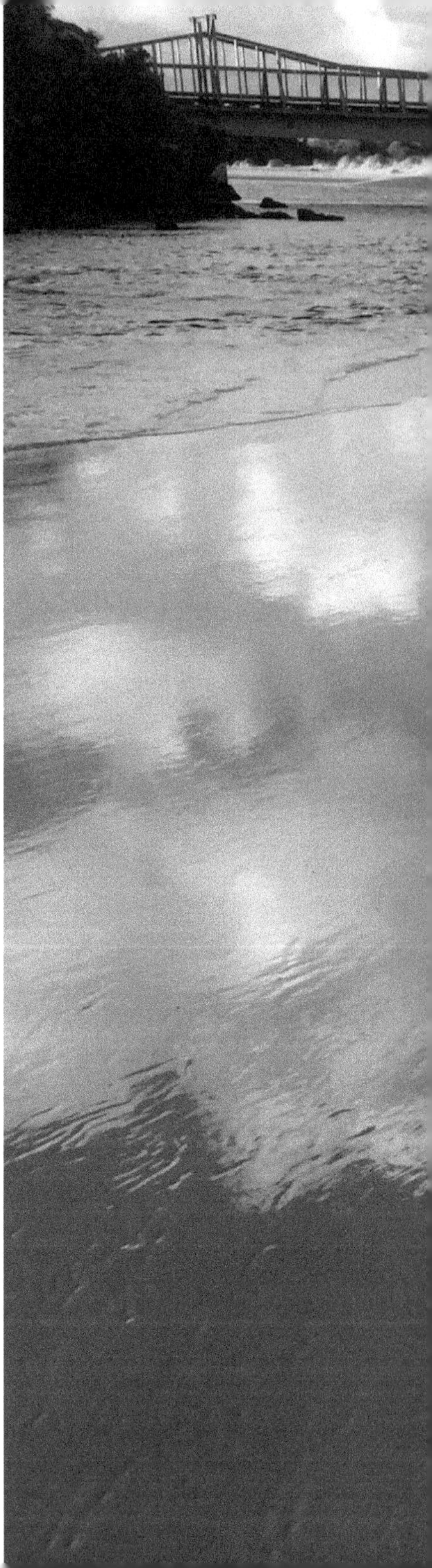

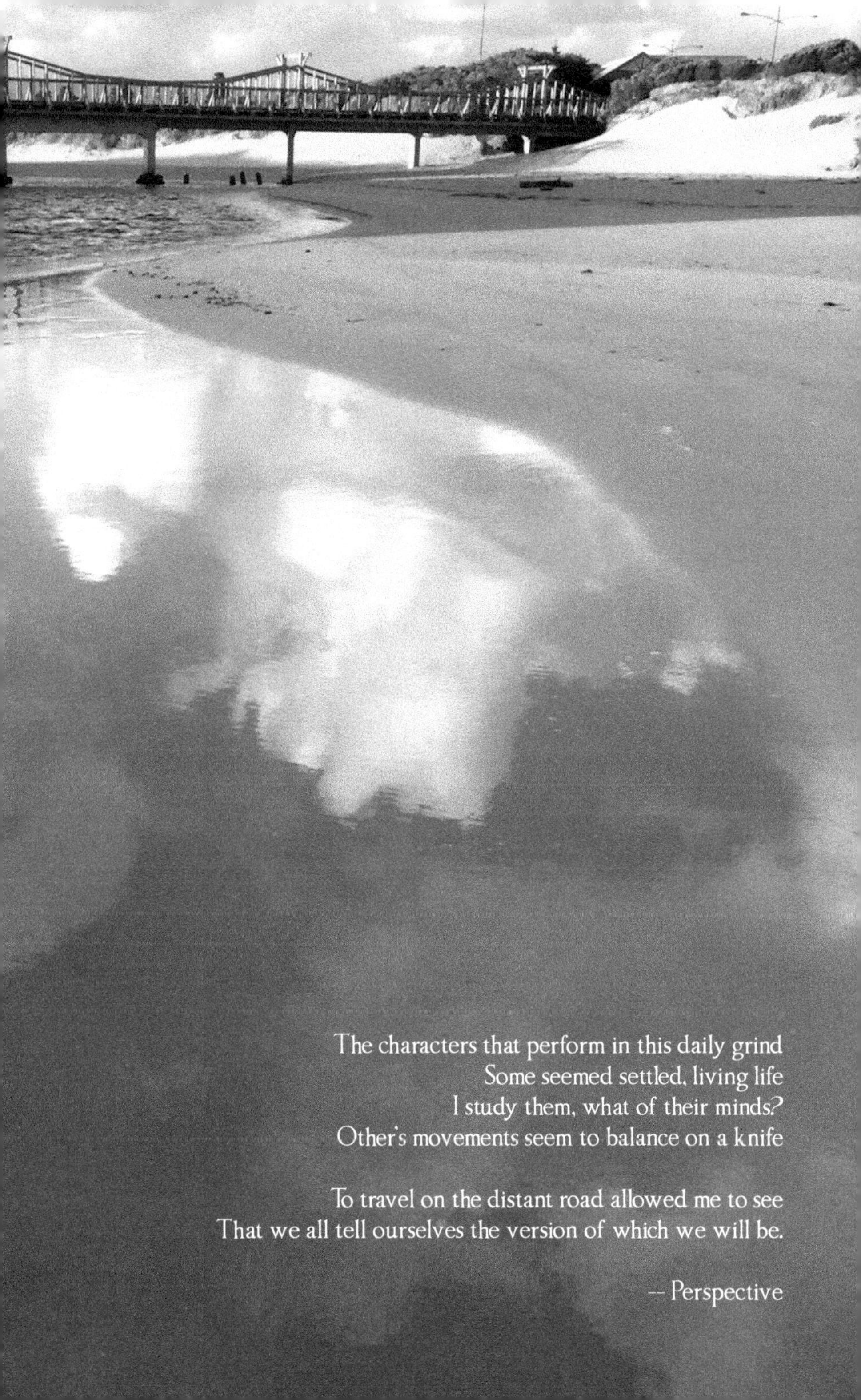

The characters that perform in this daily grind
Some seemed settled, living life
I study them, what of their minds?
Other's movements seem to balance on a knife

To travel on the distant road allowed me to see
That we all tell ourselves the version of which we will be.

-- Perspective

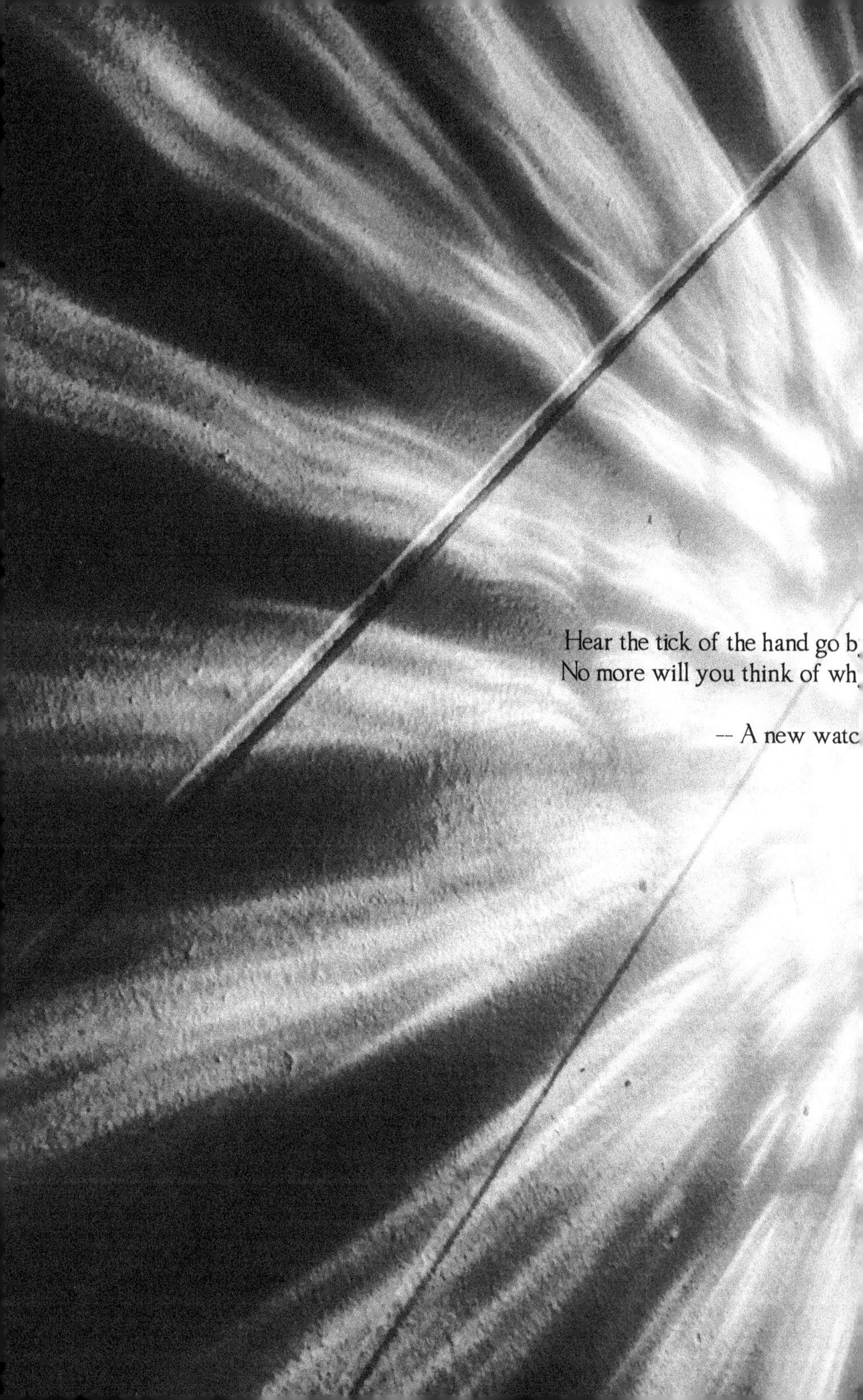

Hear the tick of the hand go b
No more will you think of wh

-- A new watc

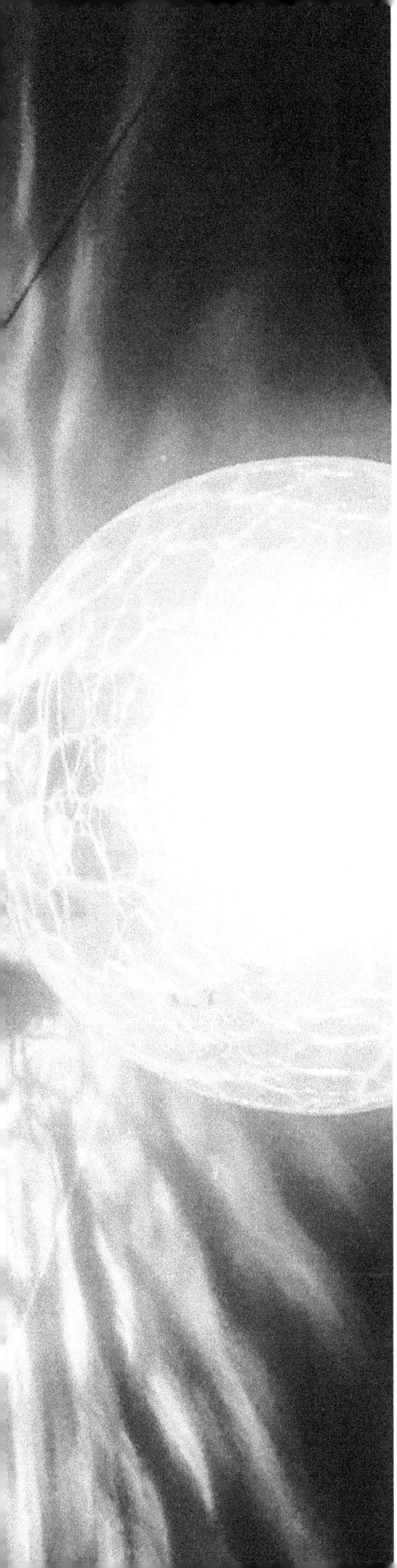

What's your perspective
For your inner thoughts
Determines your underlying self
What do you recall
Of what happened today
Which chapter did you read
In all of your greed
With the balancing times

Your mind allows such crimes

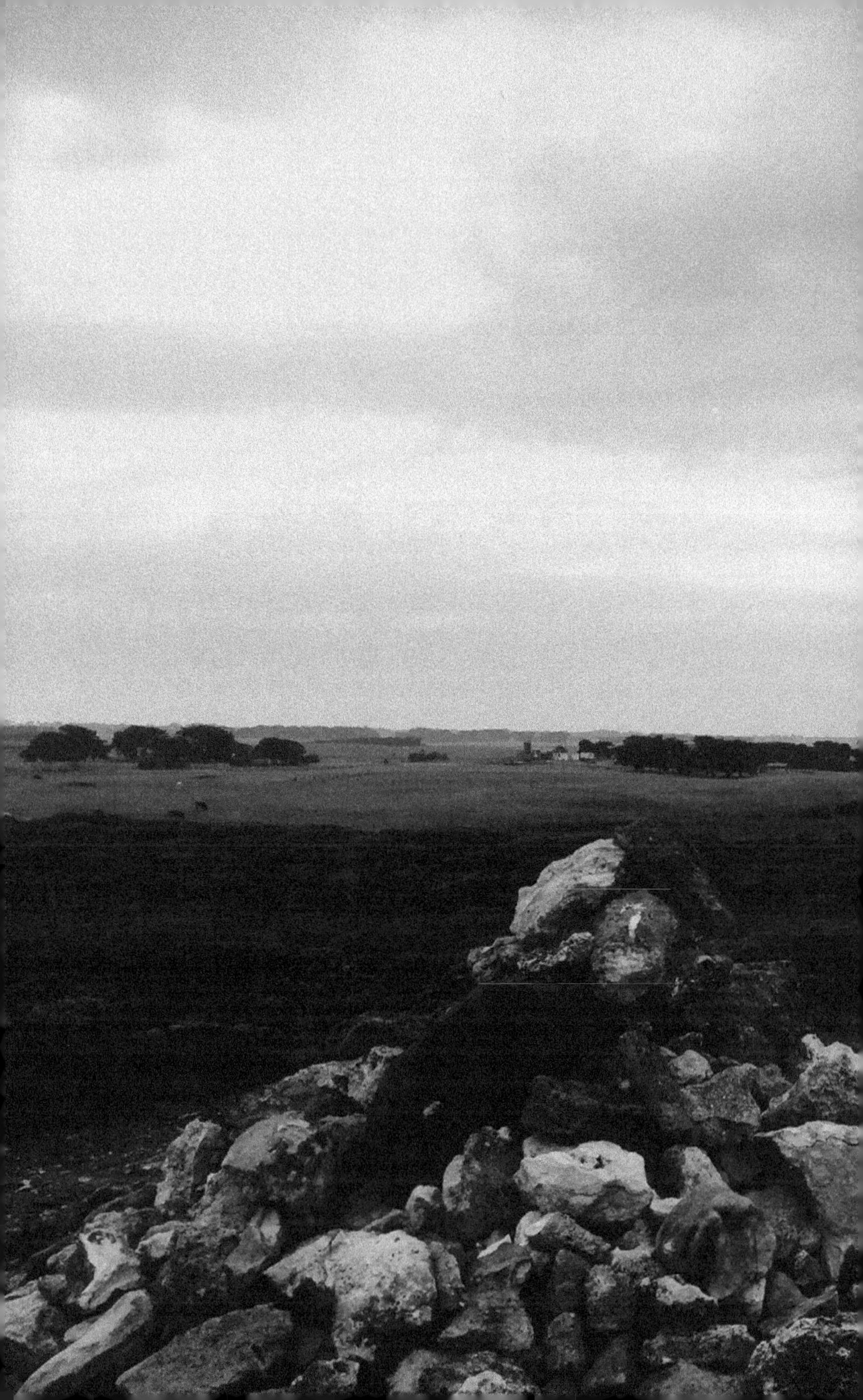

To then be awakened with an intensive care
To help you and guide you when you could not bare

To awaken the parts of you that are intrinsic and deep
To navigate your now life's shape which seems steep

— Sometimes they were mountains

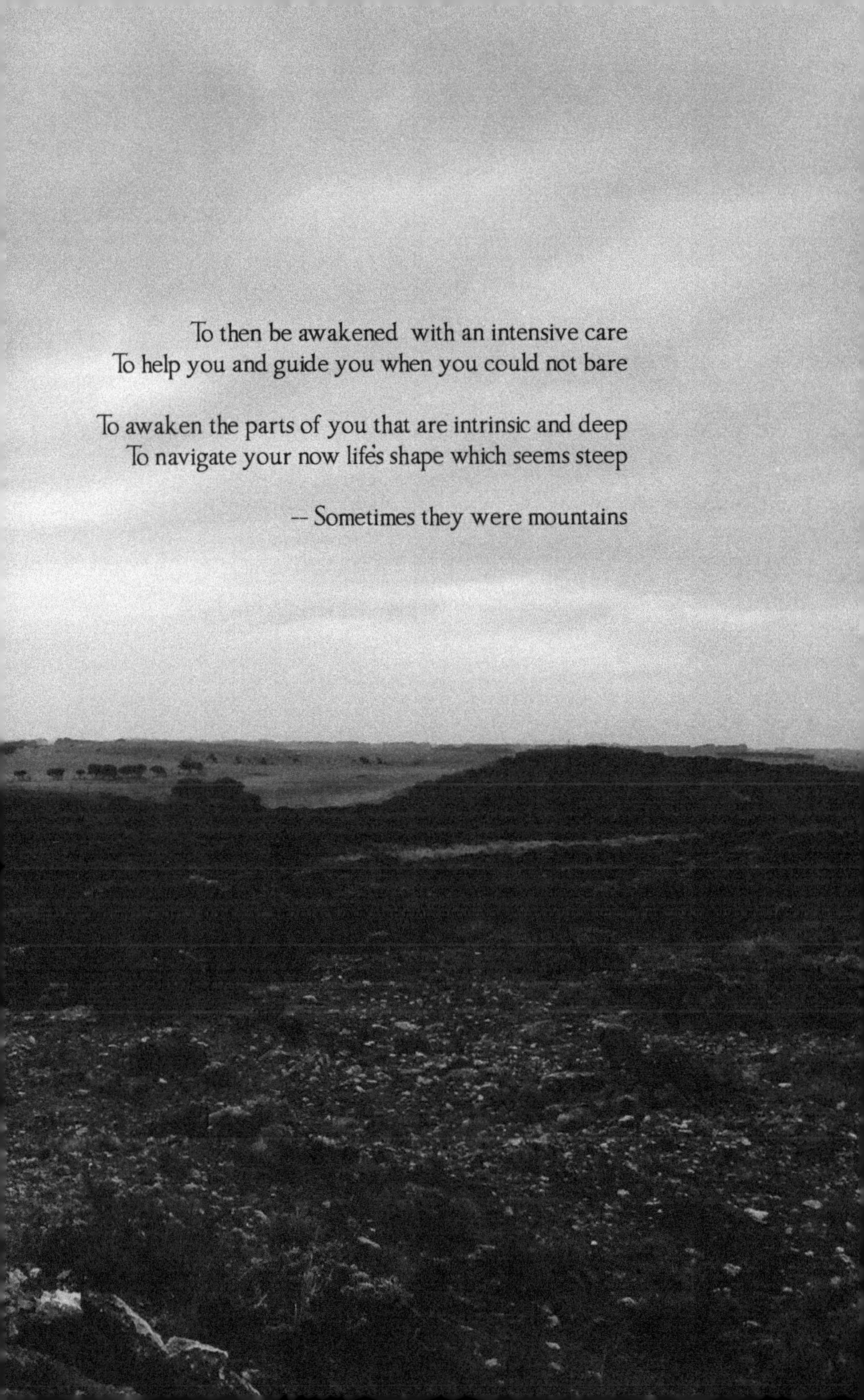

What dreams will it send or is it finally spent?
Arise now from the deep basement of despair
For when were you told your life would be fair?

-- We compare our battle scars

What is my total worth?
Has it been released since my birth?
I sat and tallied my income and expenses
Only to realise I've jumped over far too many fences
We worked through my assets and liabilities
My worth is not my pay cheque

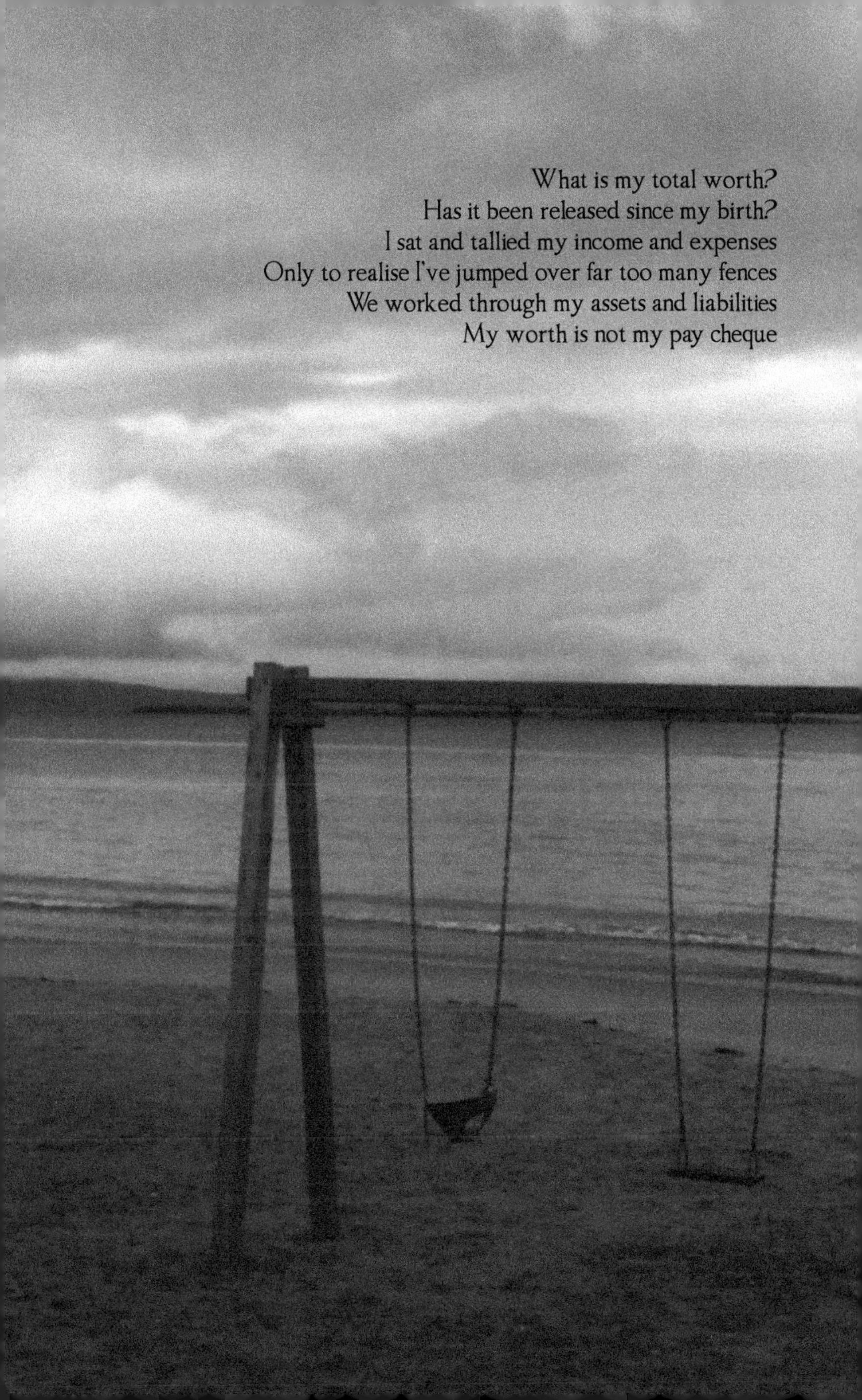

Why walk the earth to gain a net worth?
How will you be defined
from the timeline of your birth?
Will you be assessed on what you accrue?

-- Value

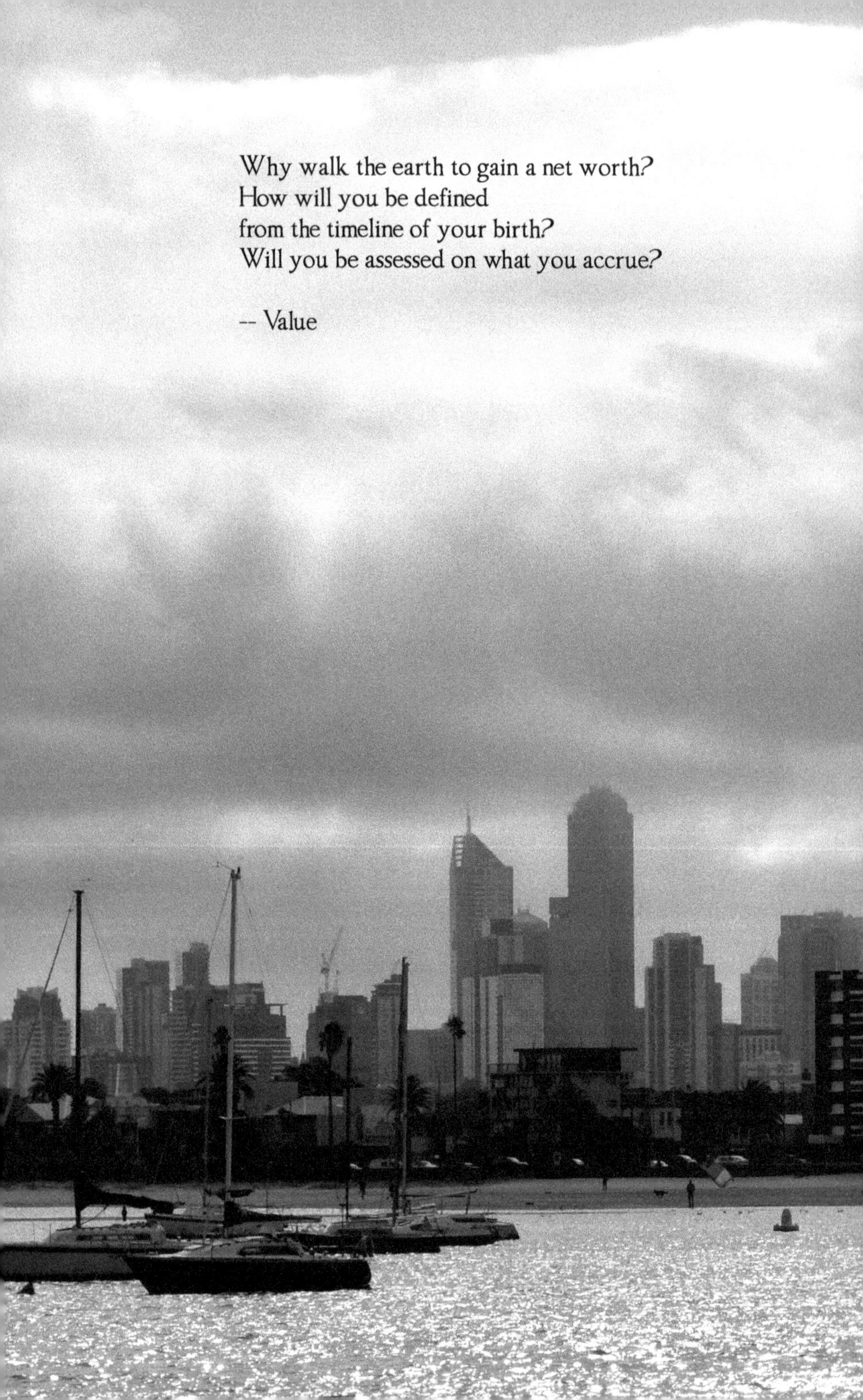

Why not walk in a community where people care?
To know of all they share
They do not seek more than what they can use

They have nothing but their lives to lose
For even maggots who feed on a carcass have a role

Material nothingness, it demands a toll

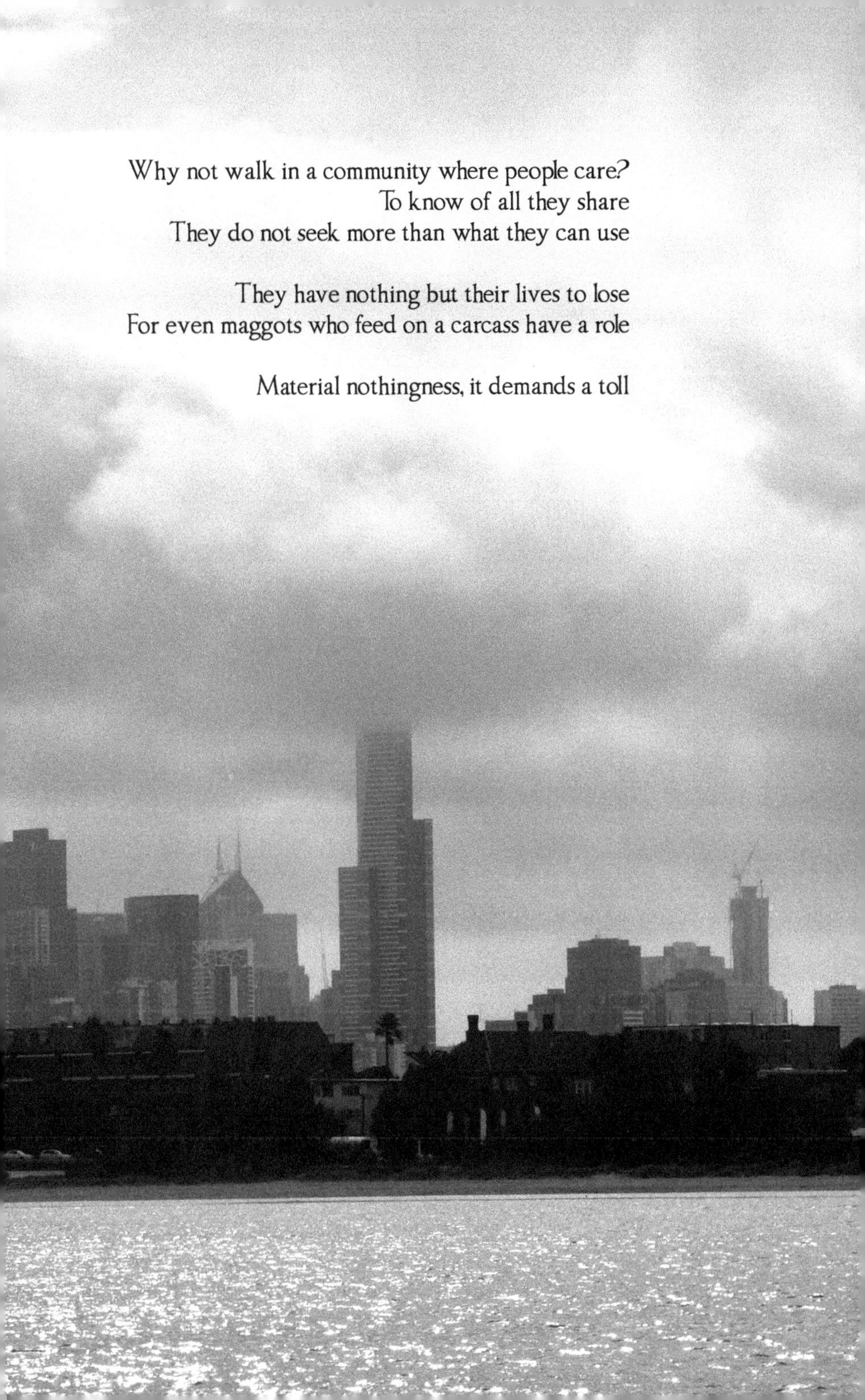

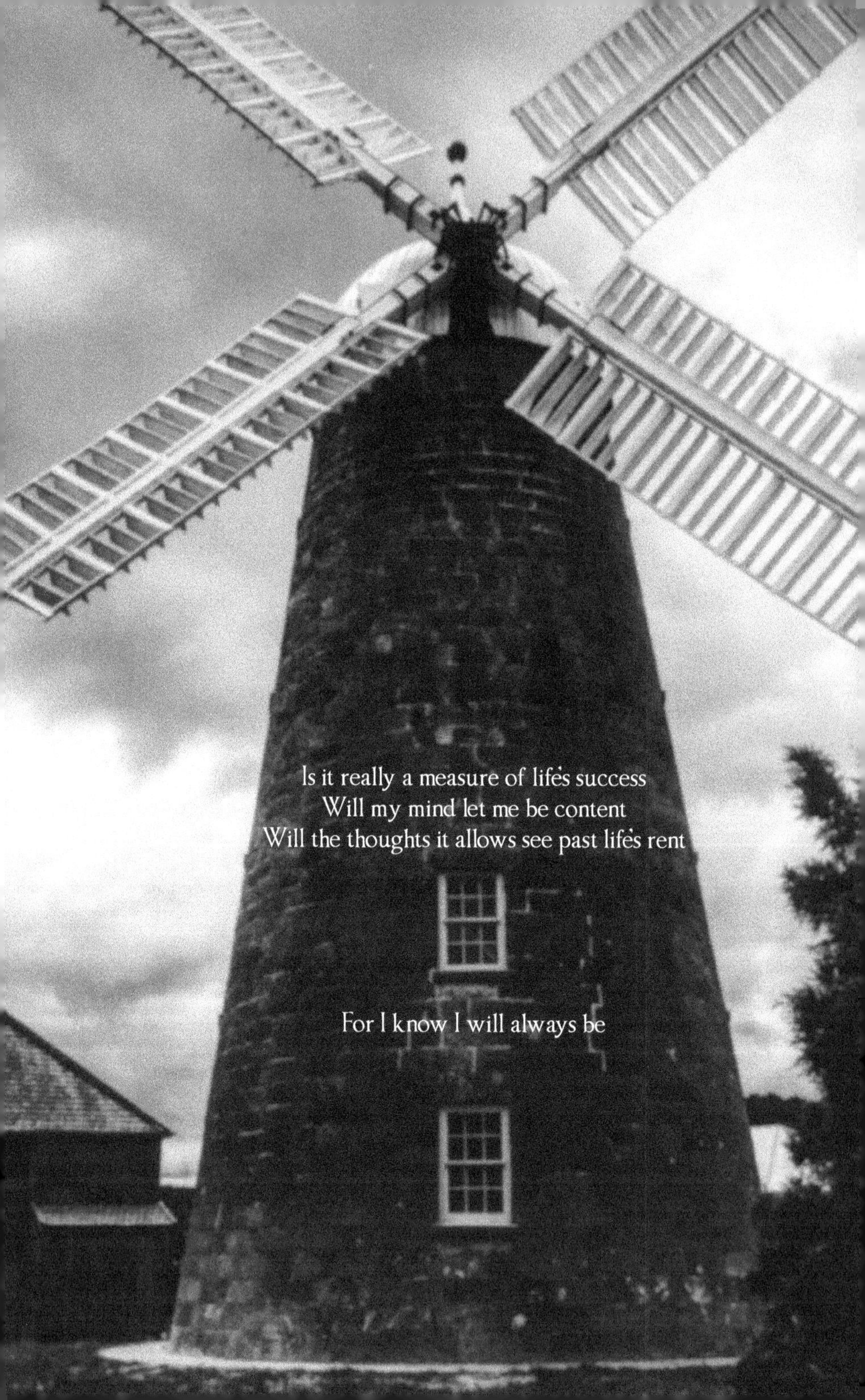

Is it really a measure of life's success
Will my mind let me be content
Will the thoughts it allows see past life's rent

For I know I will always be

To remind you of the foundation of truth
To reopen parts of you that have not reflected from youth

-- Dust in the attic

Why is it when I look inside?
I see my father's eyes

For the colour we do not share
Emotions I dare not stare

But a glance in the mirror is all it takes

For my life to seem to stop and awake
Looking through my green portal to see
What maybe I don't want to be

Why do my eyes take me there?

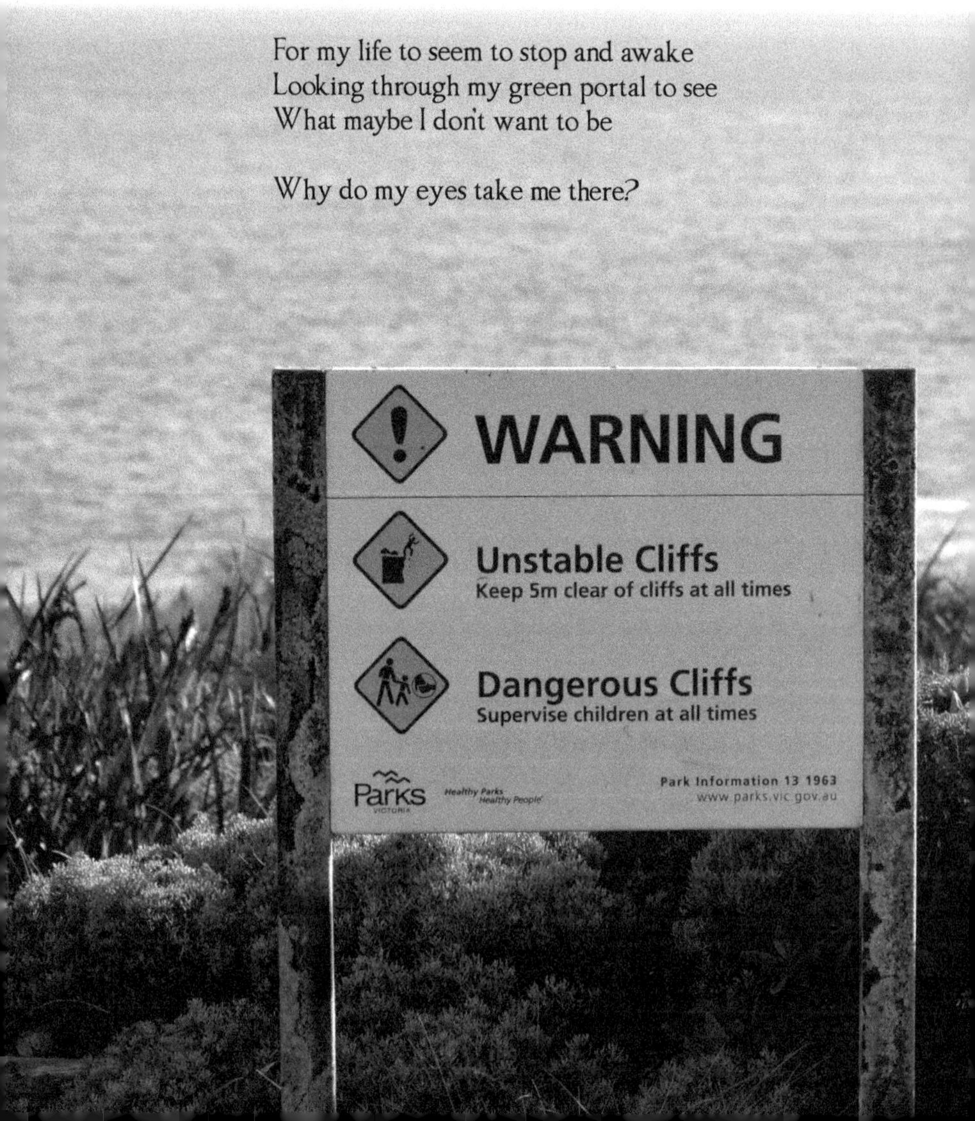

Am I testing myself for all I can bare?

-- Resistance

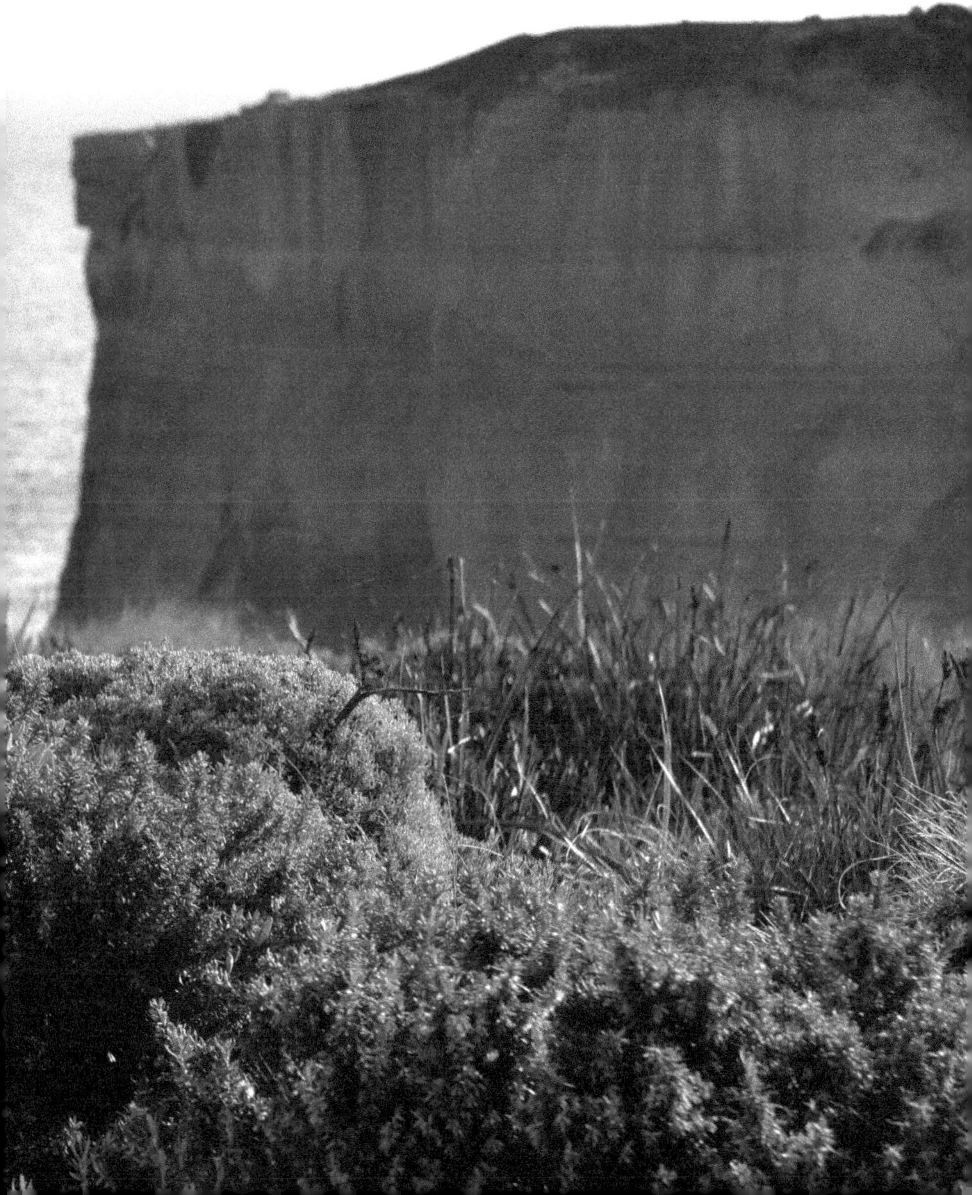

My father's eyes I have not seen
A part of my life that has long been
What makes you a father is not defined
For none of which would be mine
A bloodline with no history
A name now totally free

Write your lies

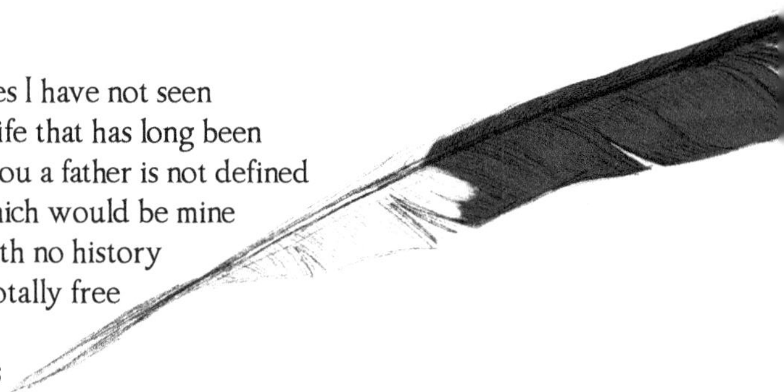

Now your history awaits for signs
One day the world will say goodbye
Will it be then that I cry?
Or will my eyes let me be
For they know of me
My father's eyes still see
But he will never really know me.

He will never know

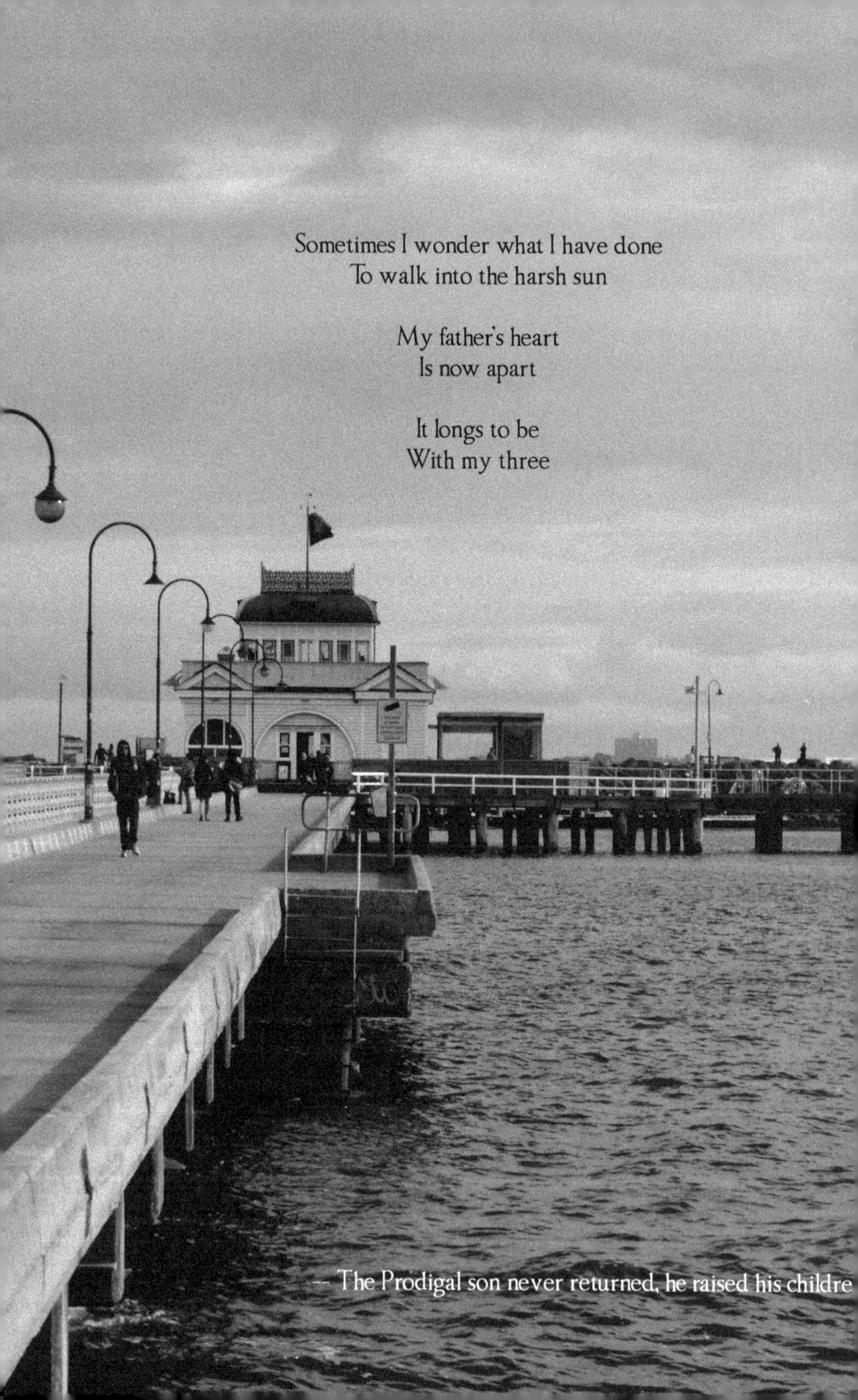

Sometimes I wonder what I have done
To walk into the harsh sun

My father's heart
Is now apart

It longs to be
With my three

-- The Prodigal son never returned, he raised his childre

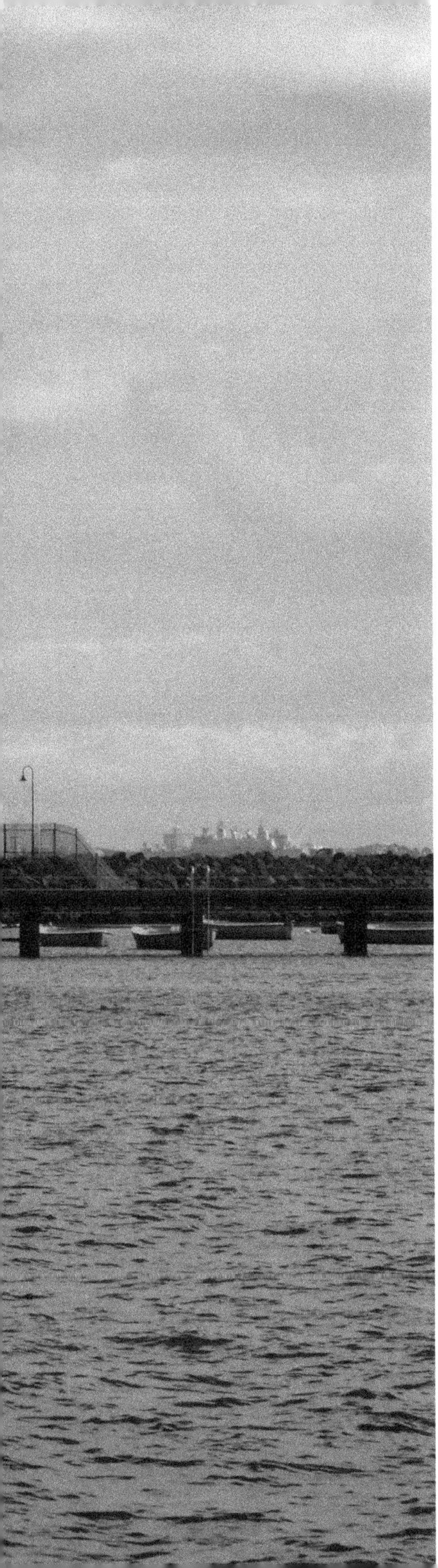

Part of me died yesterday
I need the remaining part to stay
For what would you think of me
If I only just let it be

-- Cutting threads

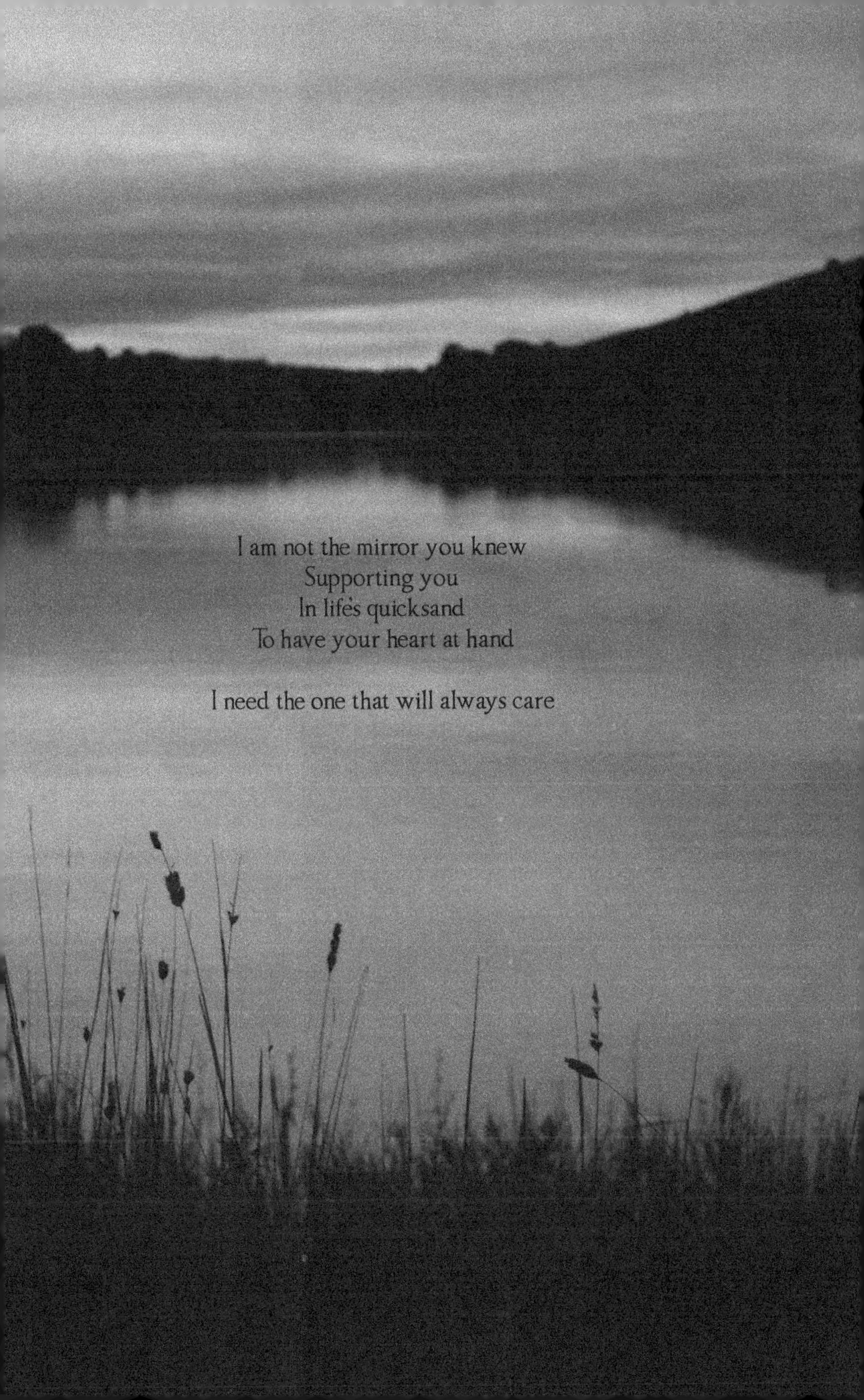

I am not the mirror you knew
Supporting you
In life's quicksand
To have your heart at hand

I need the one that will always care

Within my moment of time.
I let the outside world in
Let me hear the magpies sing

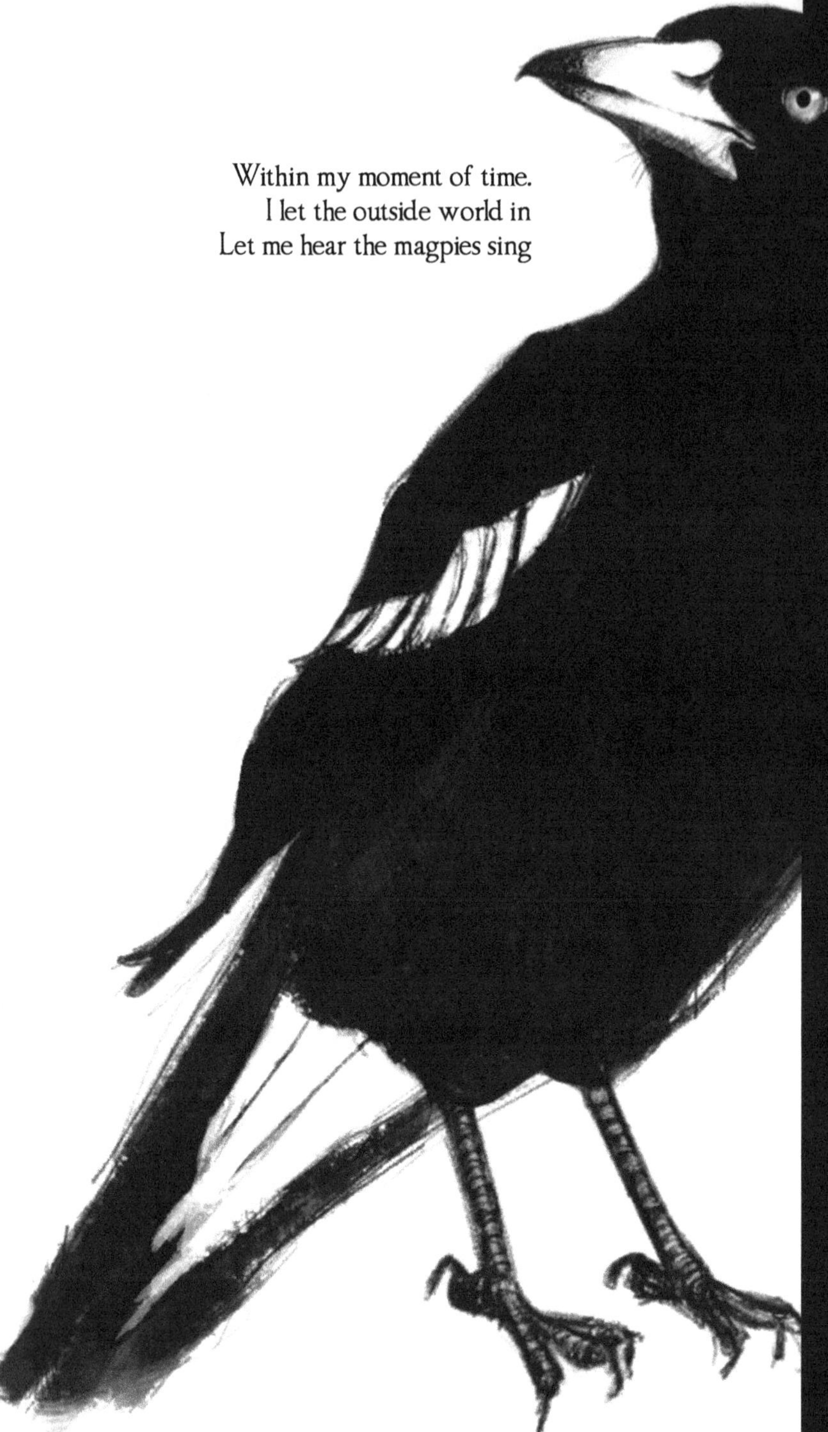

Your moment in time
How long were you guided?
Did you just sense fear?
What messages did you hear?

It frustrated me

I heard the traffic's call
I opened the door
That is truly mine
My moment in time
Our moment in time

It has passed

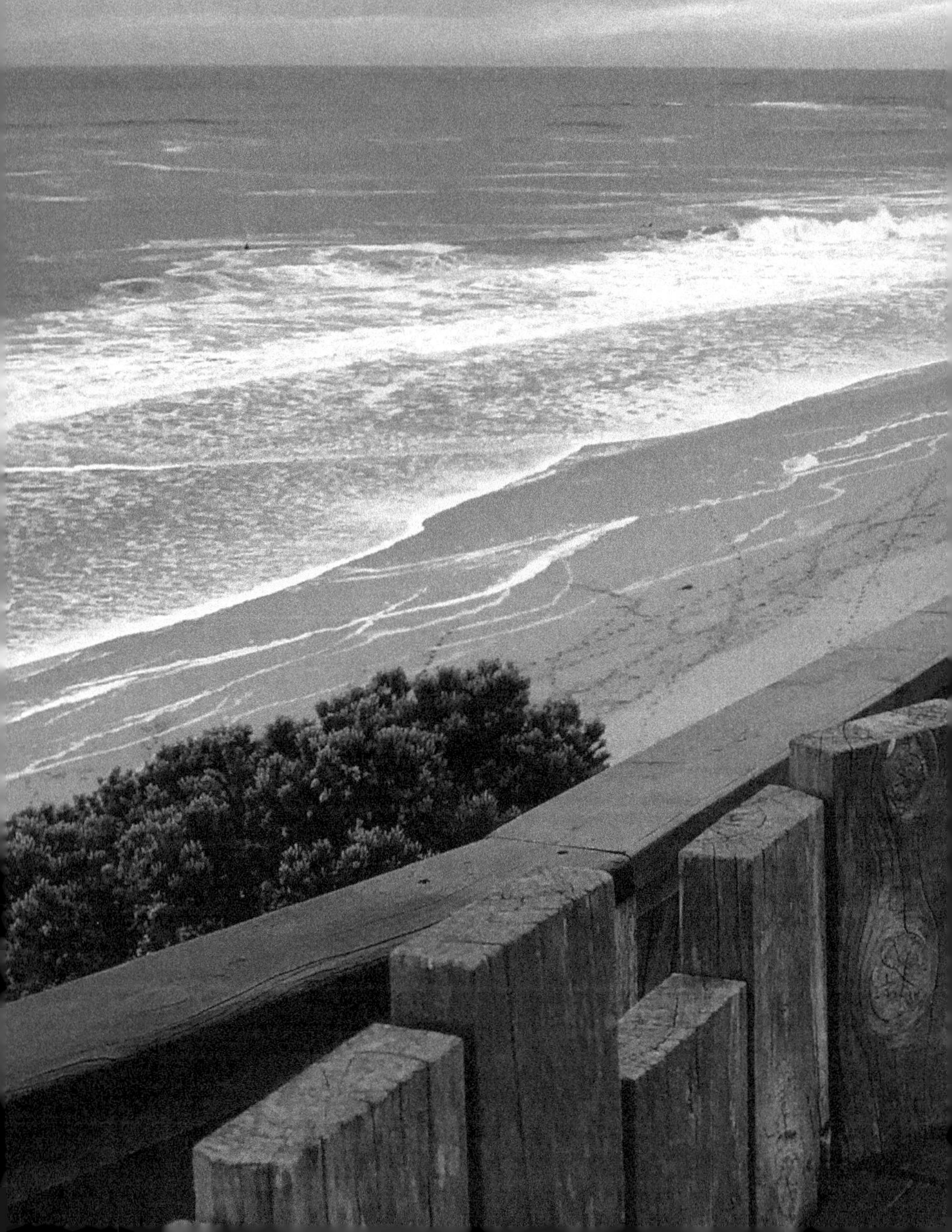

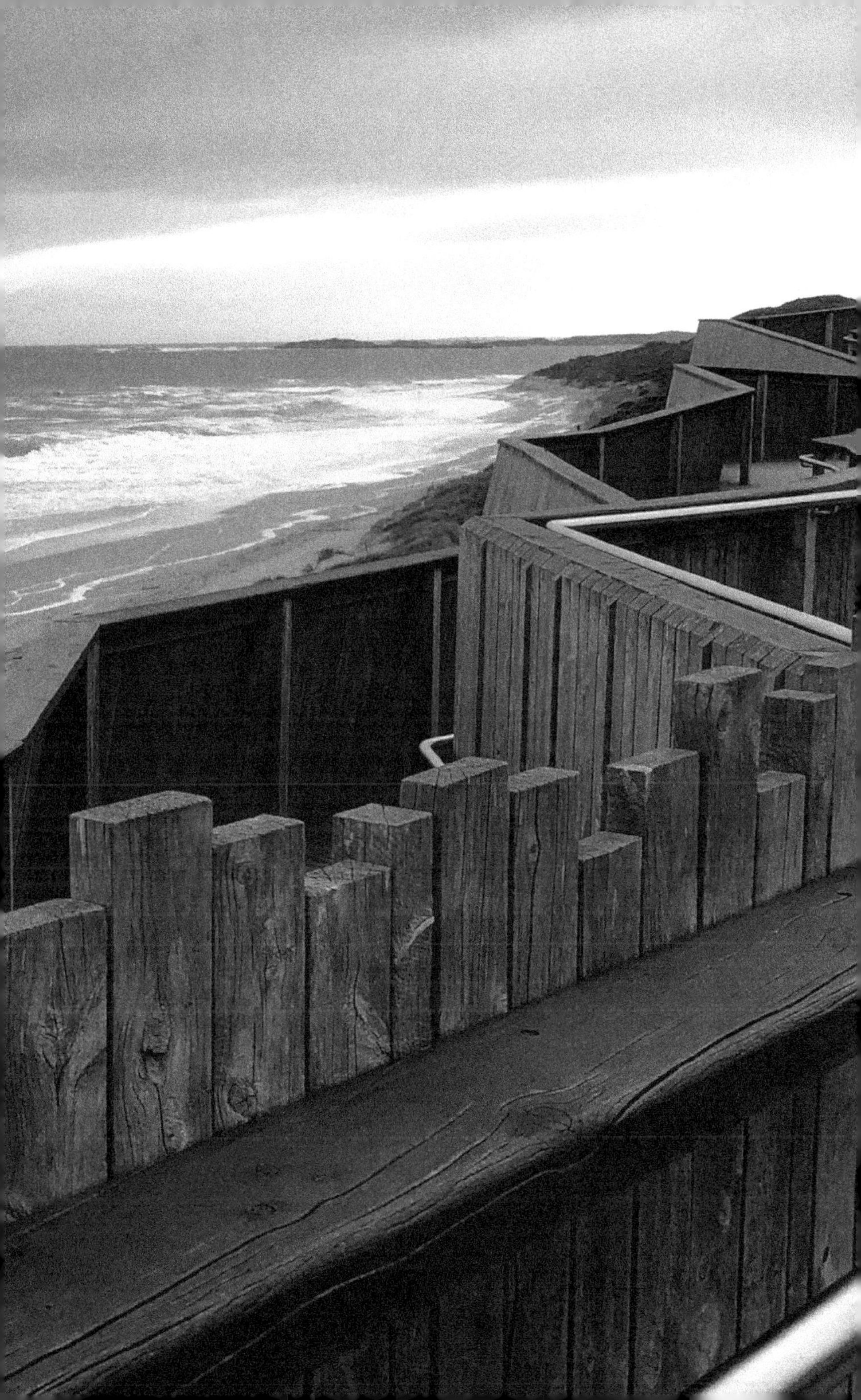

Who would ever know
Whether to draw life's bow
Or to cut ties

-- To listen in time

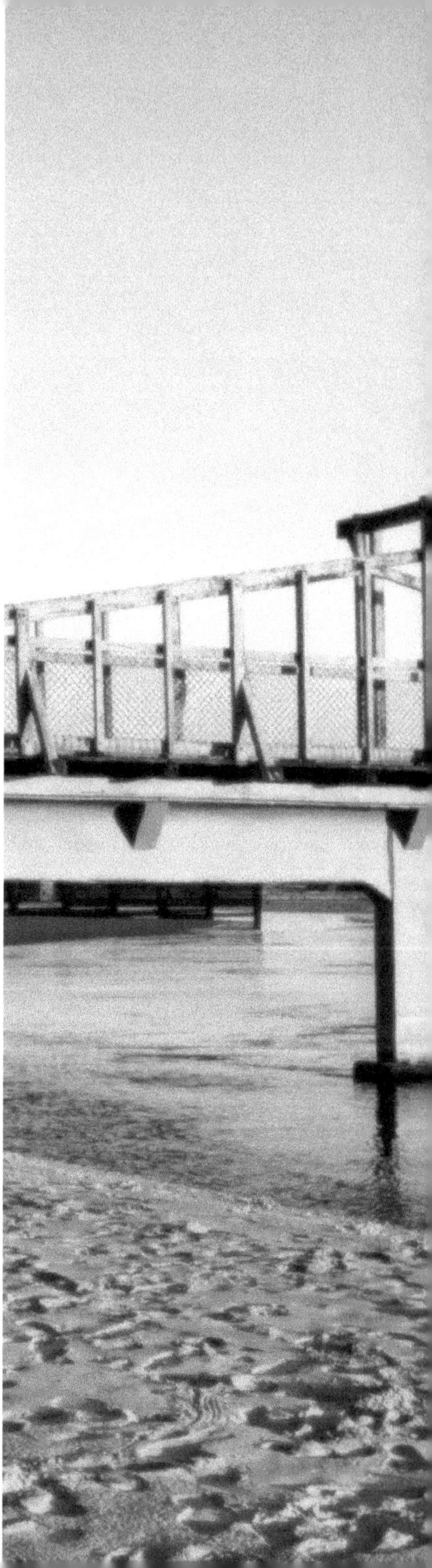

Starved of human touch
The new world seems so unforgiving
1.5m seems too far away

The world is awake to a new way of life
People have passed
We remember the fallen

Pay our respect
They were ours

A husband, a mother, a daughter, a brother, a Nonna and a Nonno

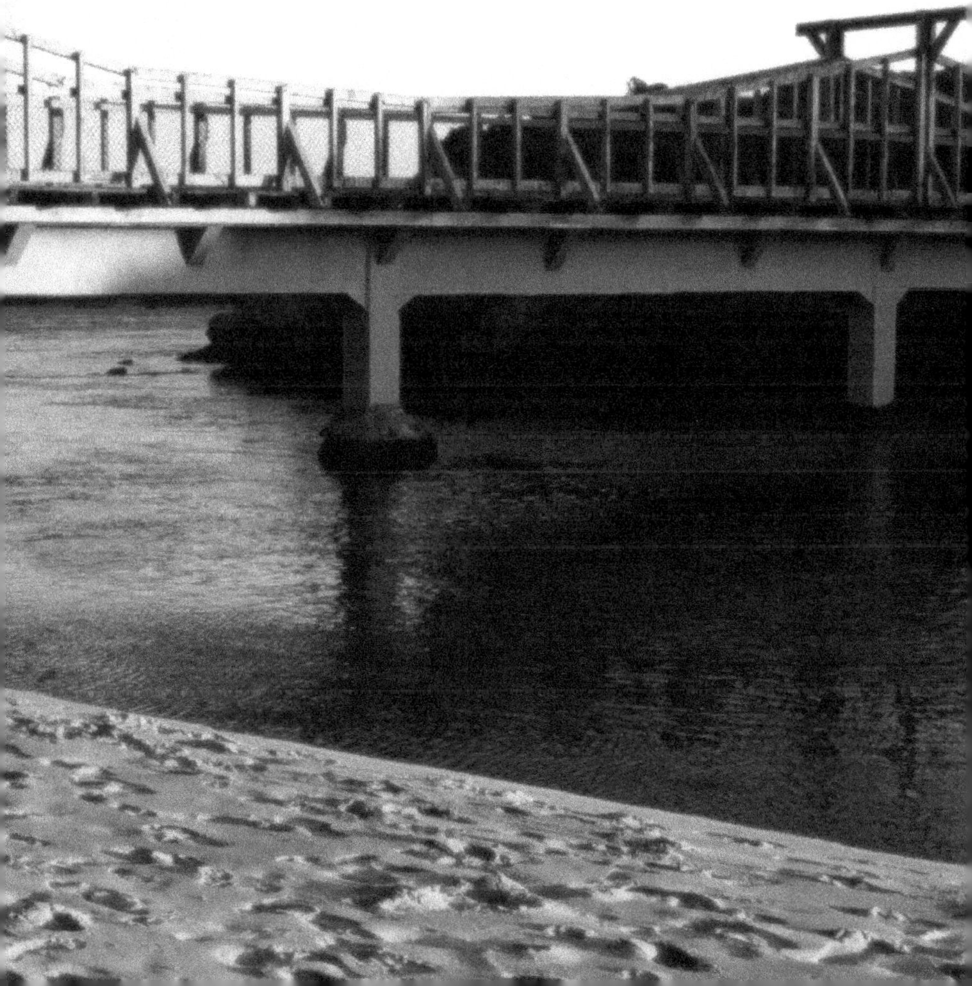

"U the HUMAN"
Our modern life of intense change
Technology is evolving
Artificial intelligence craves

A connection

We need to pause
Feel the energy of our universe
What surrounds the human mind
To become U the HUMAN

-- Our fate

Who do I want to be?
My mind won't let me be

There is a sadness in my heart
Who do I want to be?

Not knowing is killing me
The question will not go away

I know I desire all of life's bliss
But who do I want to be?

What will make me whole?

How will you be ready when your time approaches your sludge?

For you will be known not from your facade

But from the material nothingness that is marked on your life's card.

-- A meeting within myself

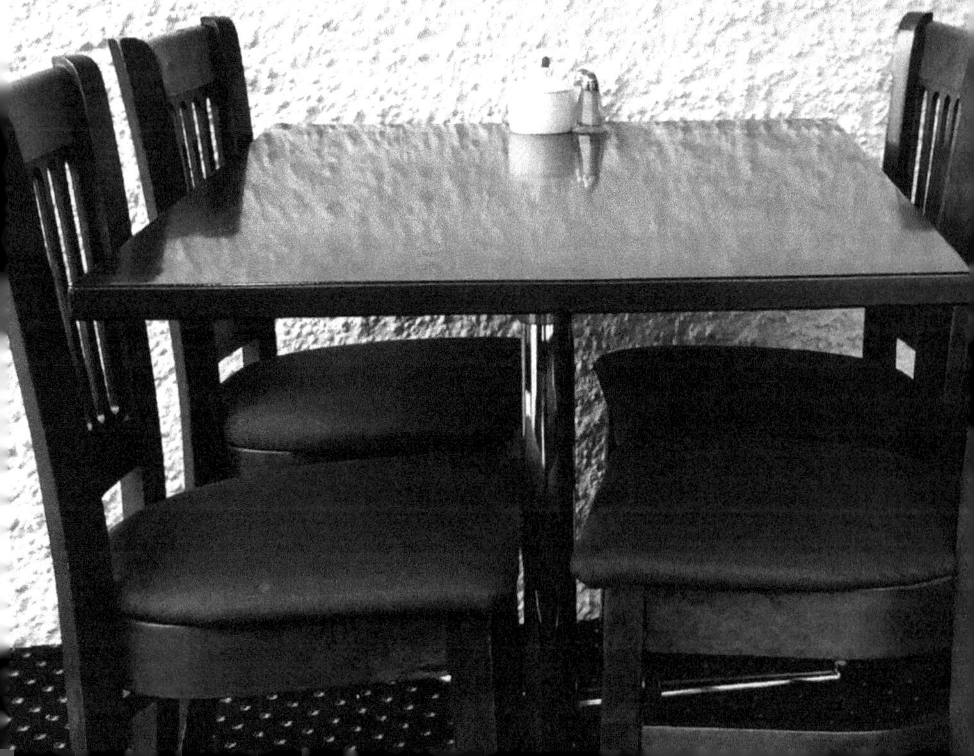

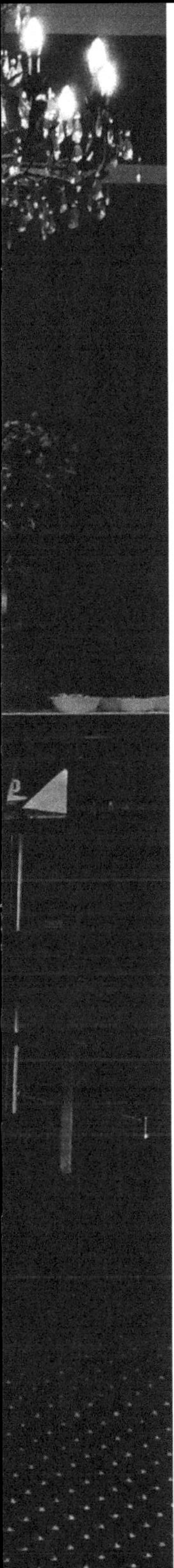

We will wake to the warmth of the sun
We need to remember
the simple pleasures
Find new ways to connect with our communities

For now be kind to the humans around you,
stay safe
and fight the pandemic

For right now our greatest weapon is to be kind.

-- To be human

I watch the door close
Where am I?
What have I done?

For when the door closes shut

For when the door closes shut

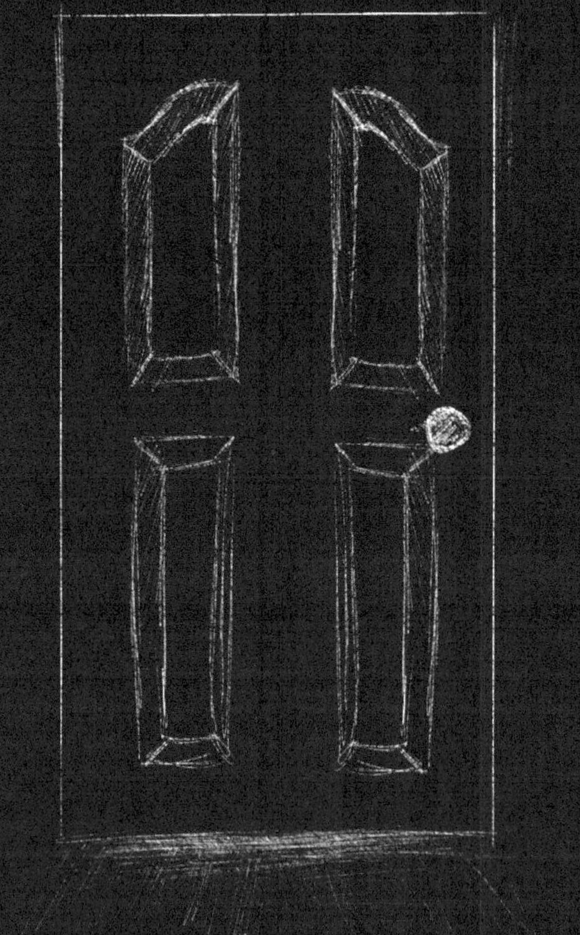

When I see my door closing

I watch every motion

Until the gaps between are shut

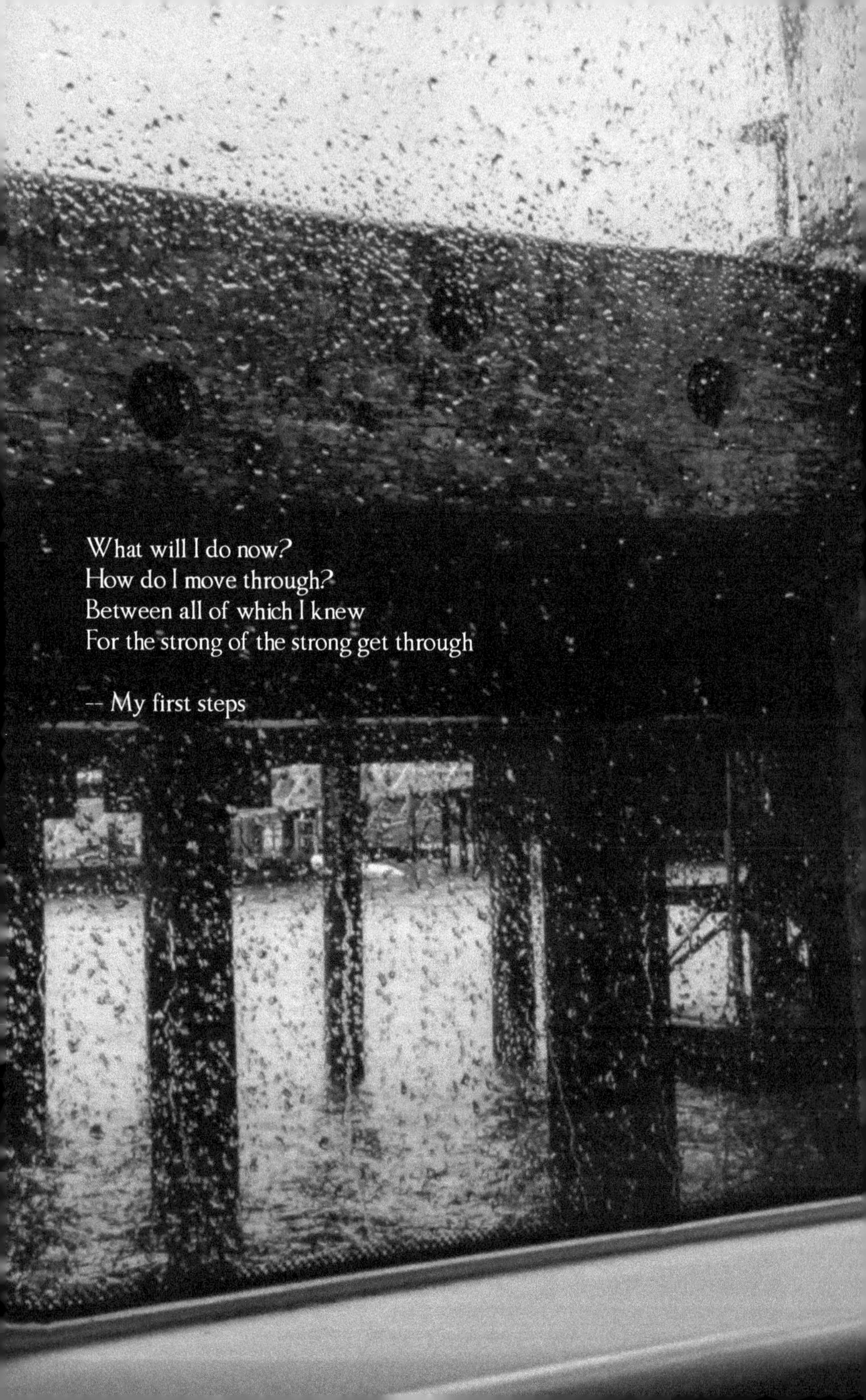

What will I do now?
How do I move through?
Between all of which I knew
For the strong of the strong get through

-- My first steps

Through the gates of the enriched life's are few
I will stand at my door and knock

I need the courage to walk through

Stand tall
And leave the door open
Allowing the wounds I've held
To remain open

-- Resilience

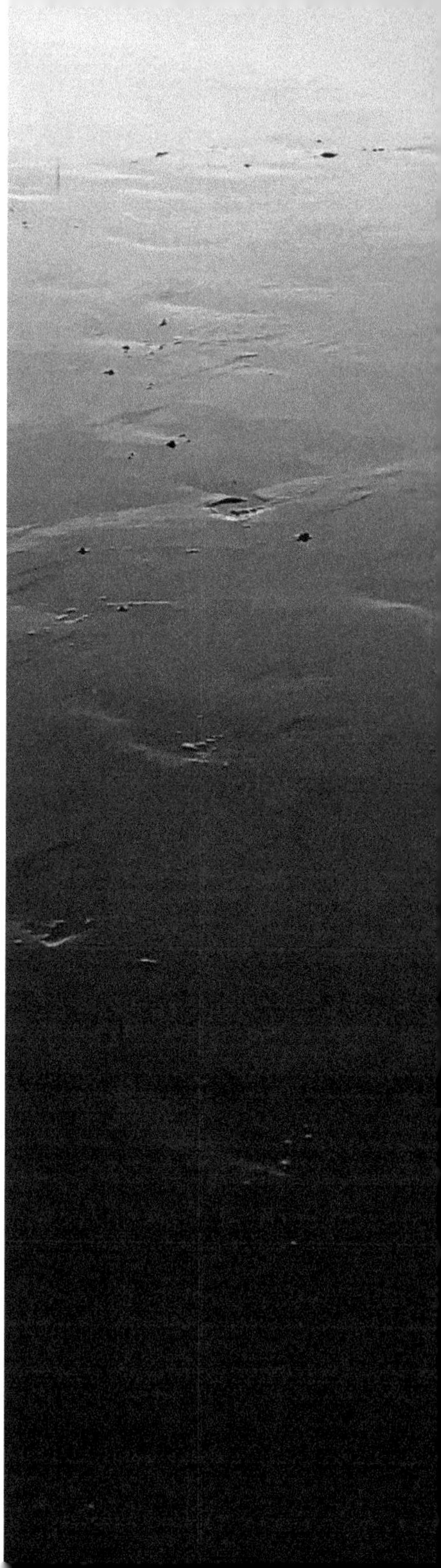

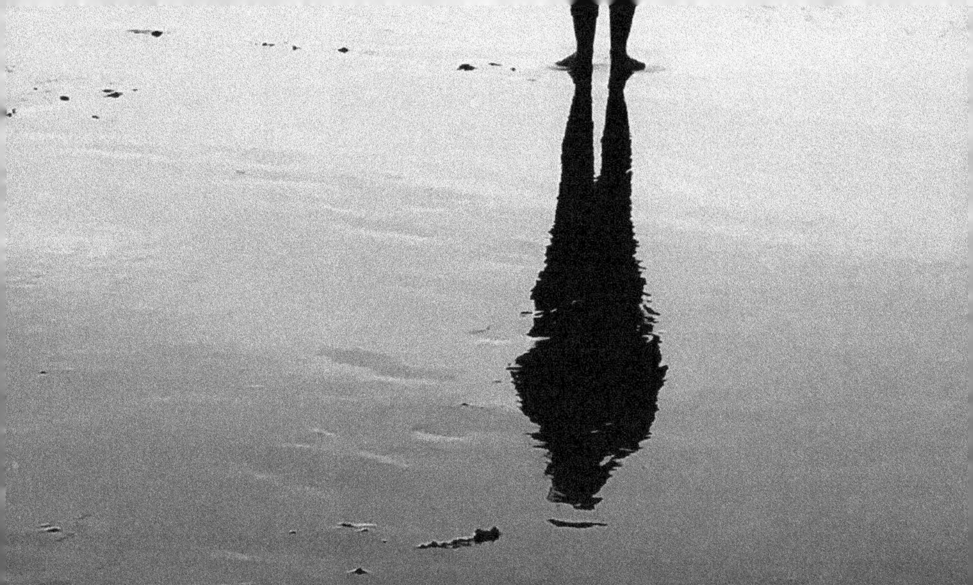

I see the reflections from lights in the sky
No more will I wonder
About the people walking
Living a life that is not passing them
What have we really found?

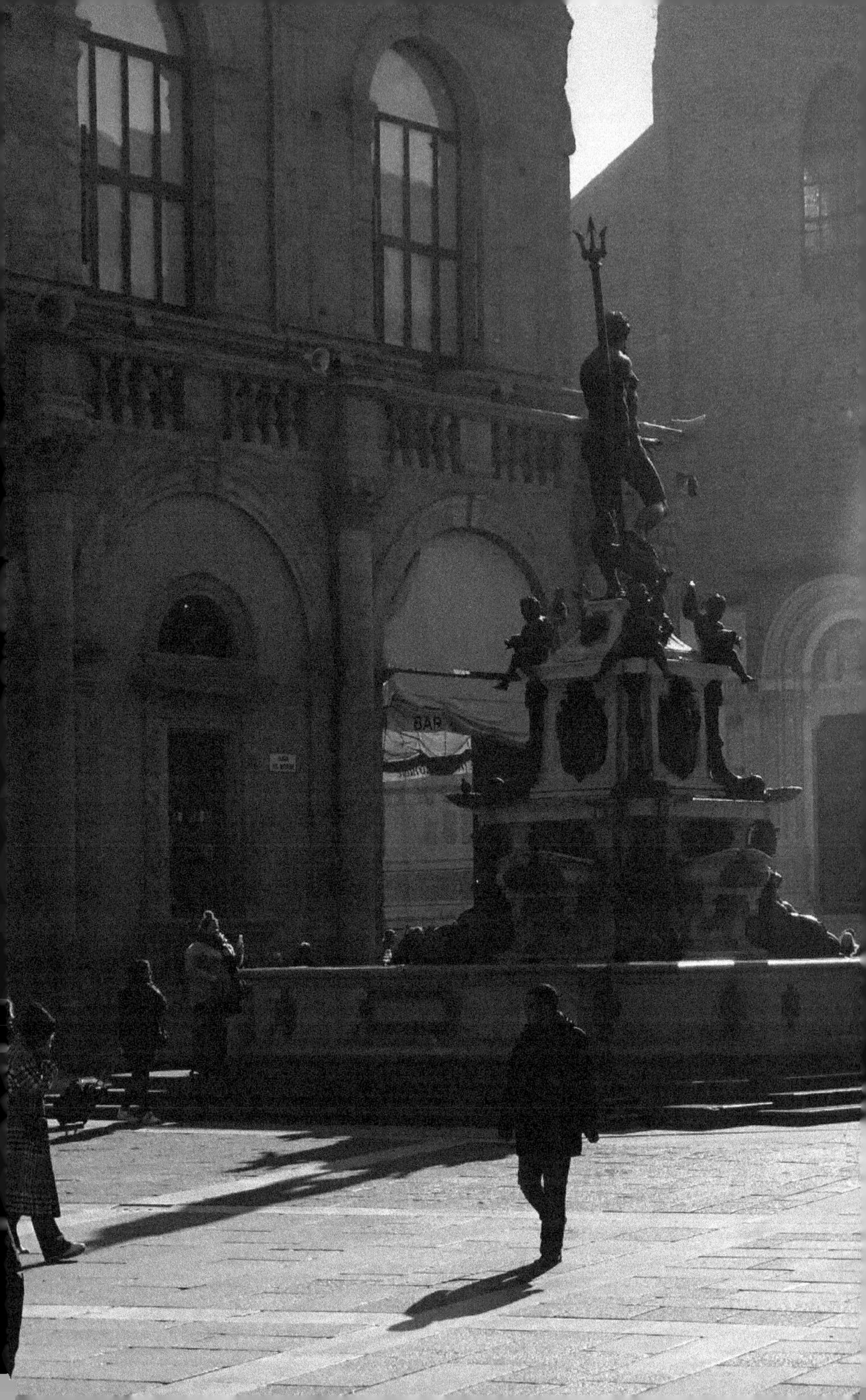
BAR

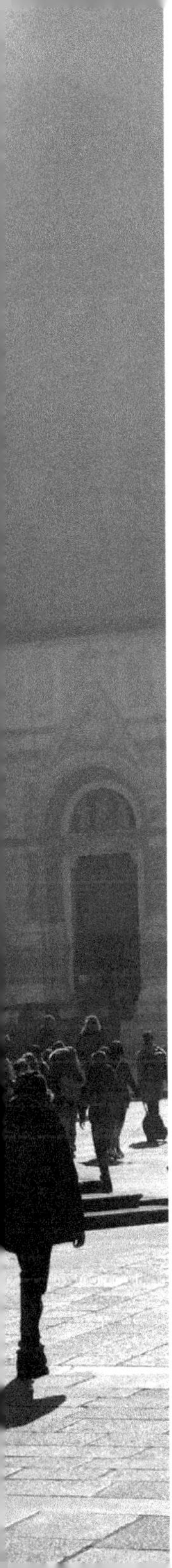

I stand before all that will listen
For my life will be defined by my character, not all that glistens
I will walk with kings and gods and judge them on their life's play
As I take my voice to the world to have my say

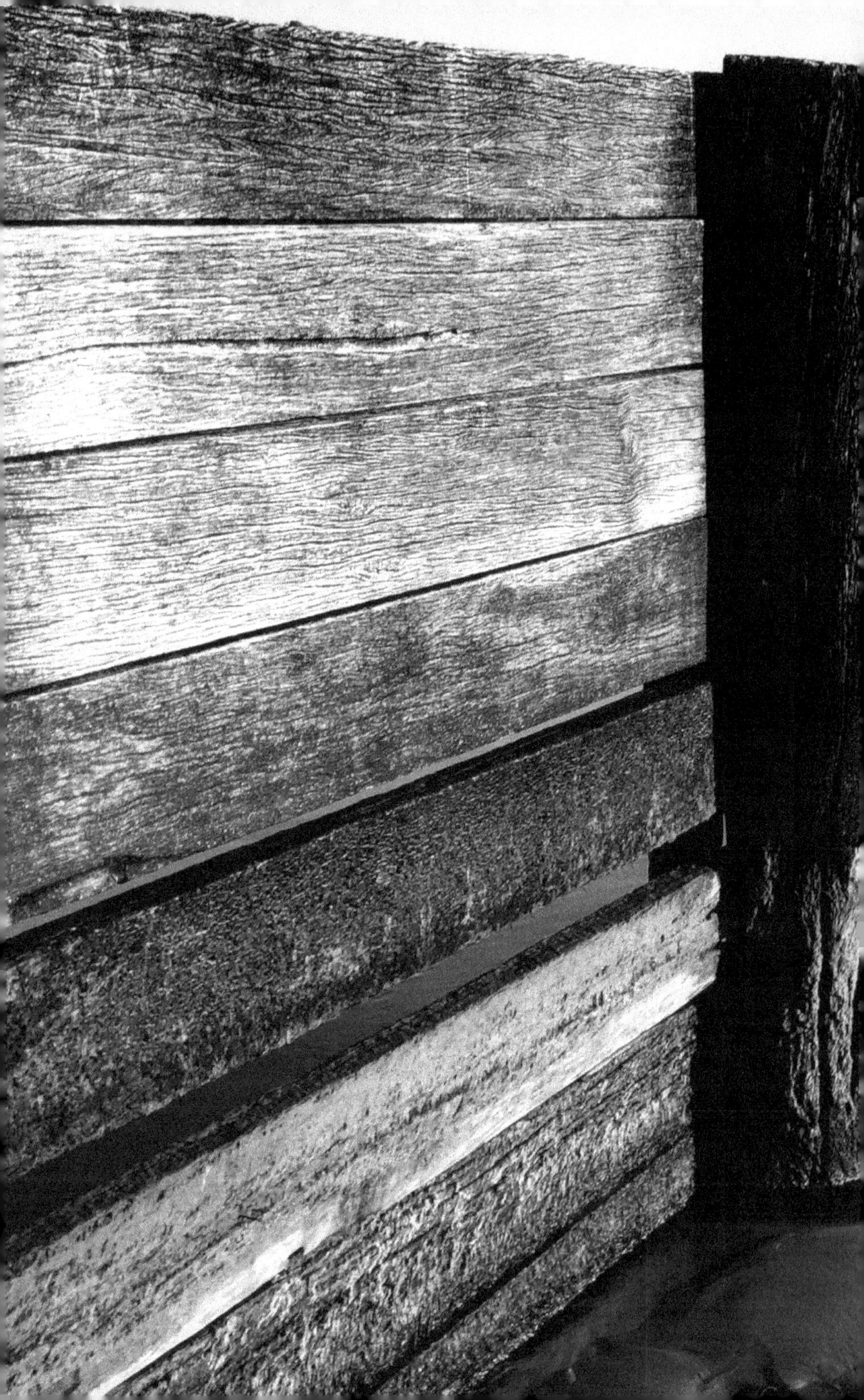

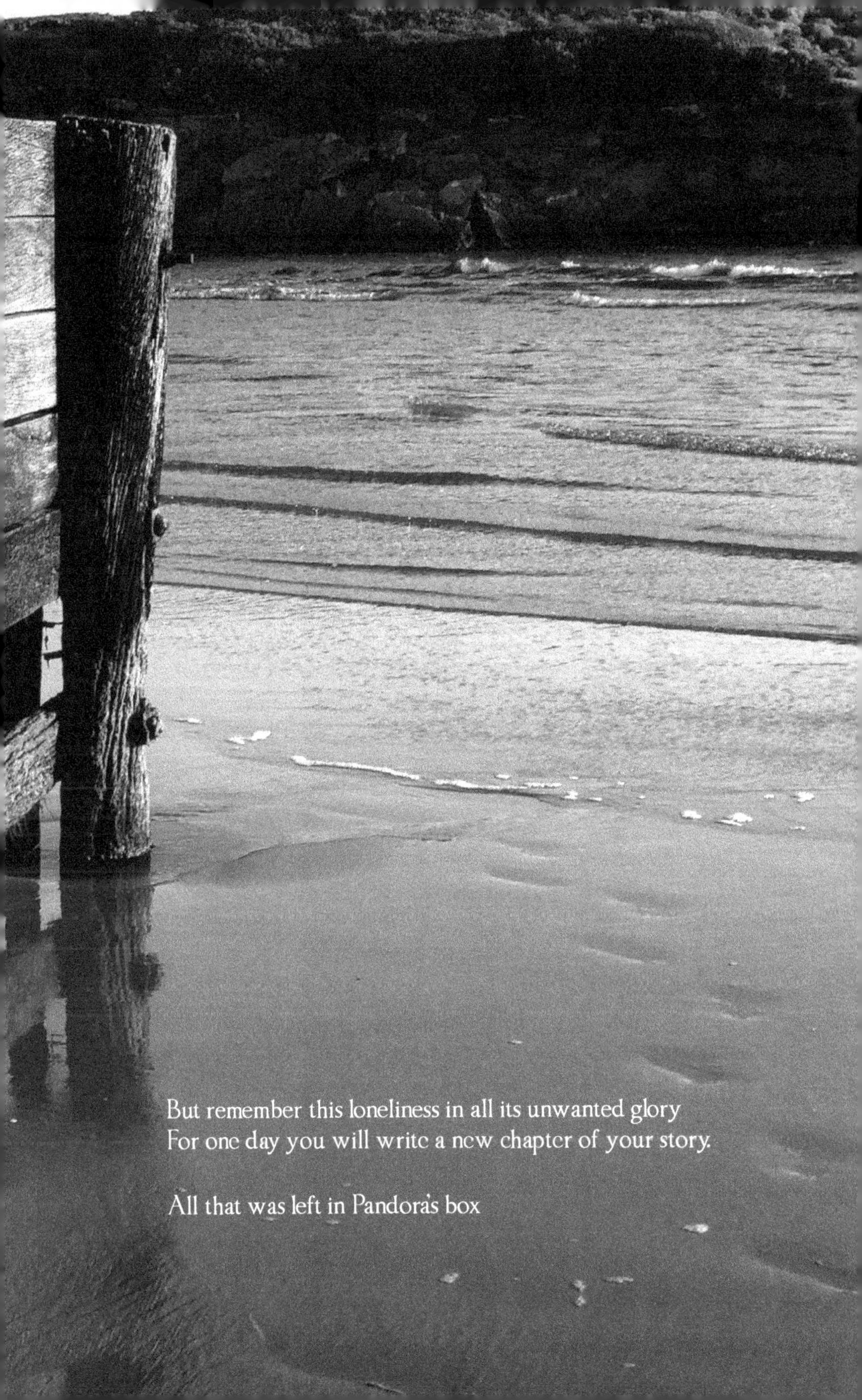

But remember this loneliness in all its unwanted glory
For one day you will write a new chapter of your story.

All that was left in Pandora's box

Staring into the abyss
I think of what I have missed
Stagnant no longer

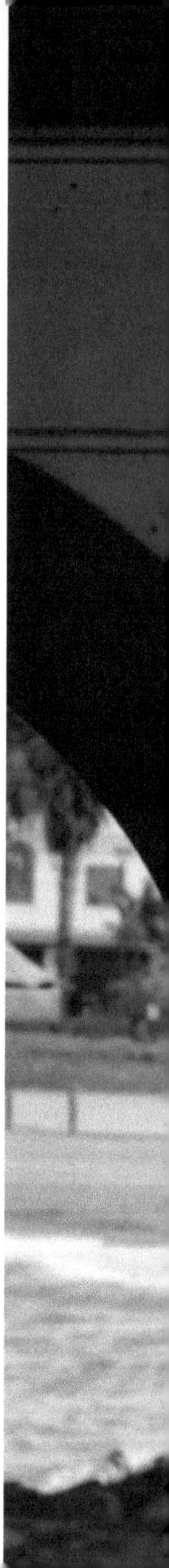

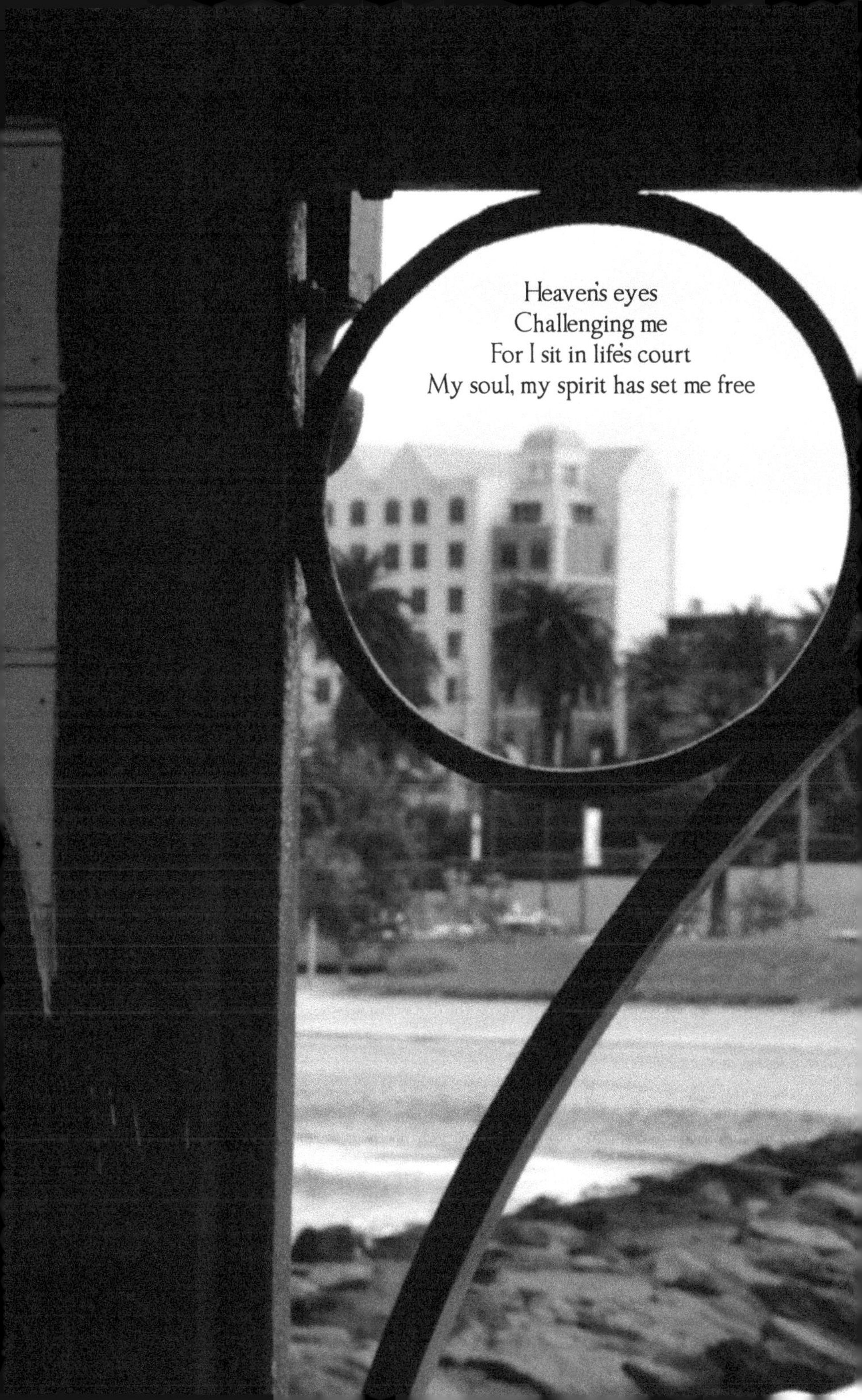

Heaven's eyes
Challenging me
For I sit in life's court
My soul, my spirit has set me free

Some would say

The Divine Goddess of life

Could alter you

Without strife

To feel love

Hidden deep within

With clear vision

You have never seen

To honour this grateful gift

Without longing

For this life's shift

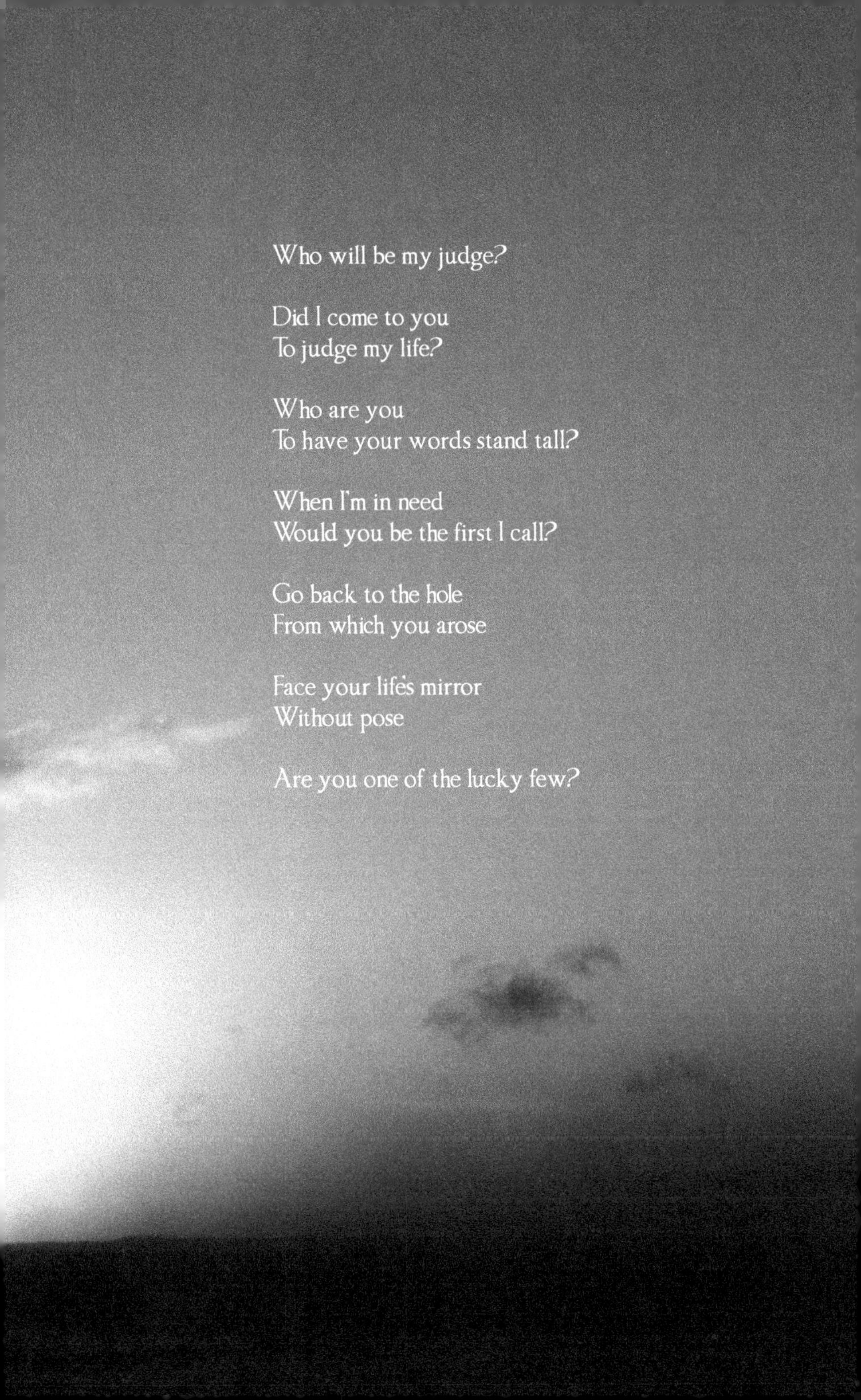

Who will be my judge?

Did I come to you
To judge my life?

Who are you
To have your words stand tall?

When I'm in need
Would you be the first I call?

Go back to the hole
From which you arose

Face your life's mirror
Without pose

Are you one of the lucky few?

I wonder if it will be 'come what may'
For who really knows who you are
When people view their vision of you from afar
Will my mind ever be content?

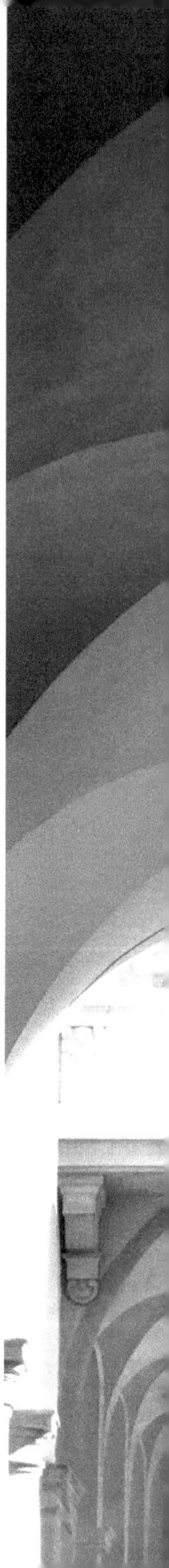

I've walked many roads and had many guides
Will you walk with me?
Will we have the courage to face the gates?
Is love by definition ever fair?
If love is around does it really care?

For what is love?

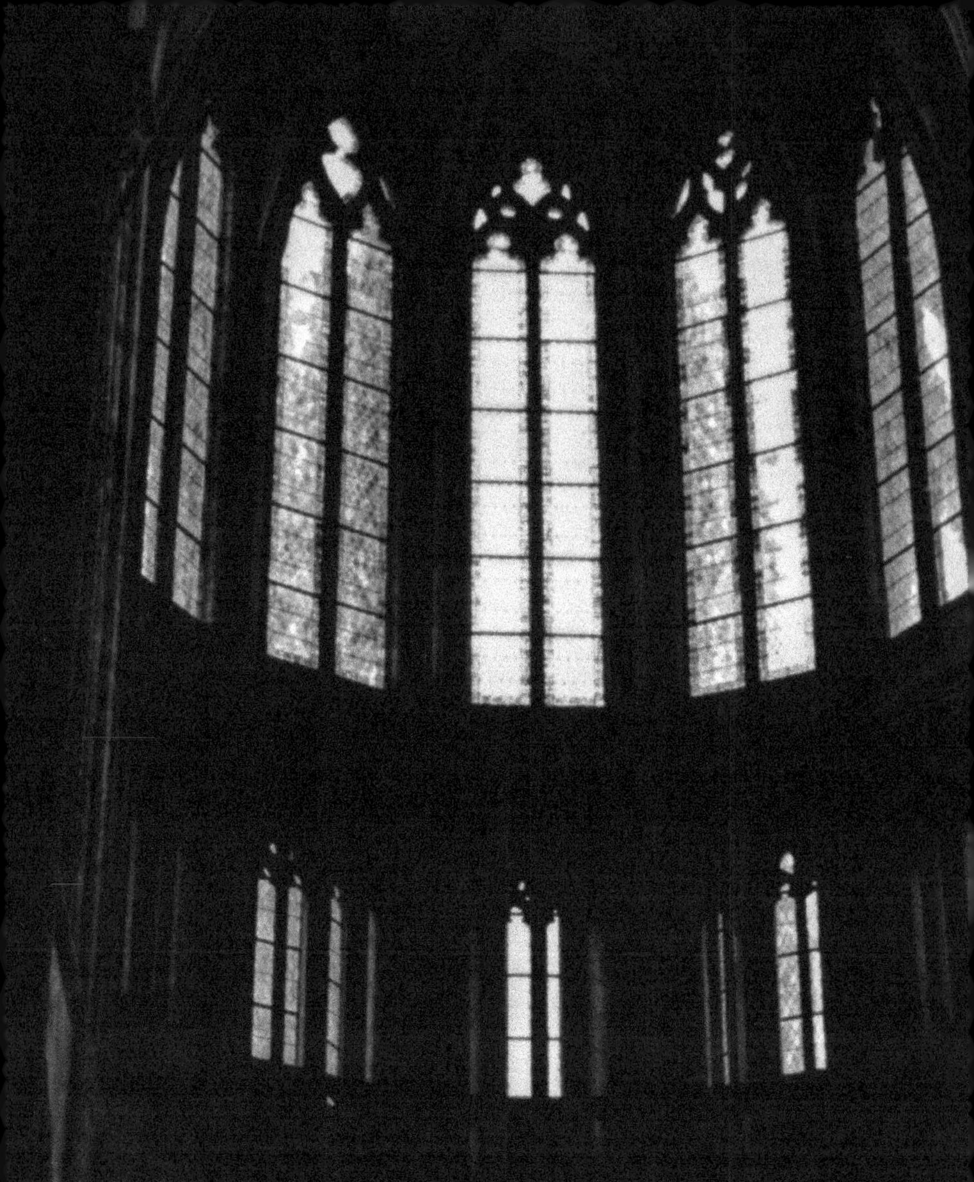

The embrace of kindness
For I walk among the people

In days gone

waiting at the steeple

We will be released

Do you ever notice the light on the leaves on the tree?
The tree that you gaze at and dream of being free

Searching for the perfection of a dove long since taken flight
To open your eyes from the darkest night

Then you are free

I sit and stare into nothing

Knowing I could be something

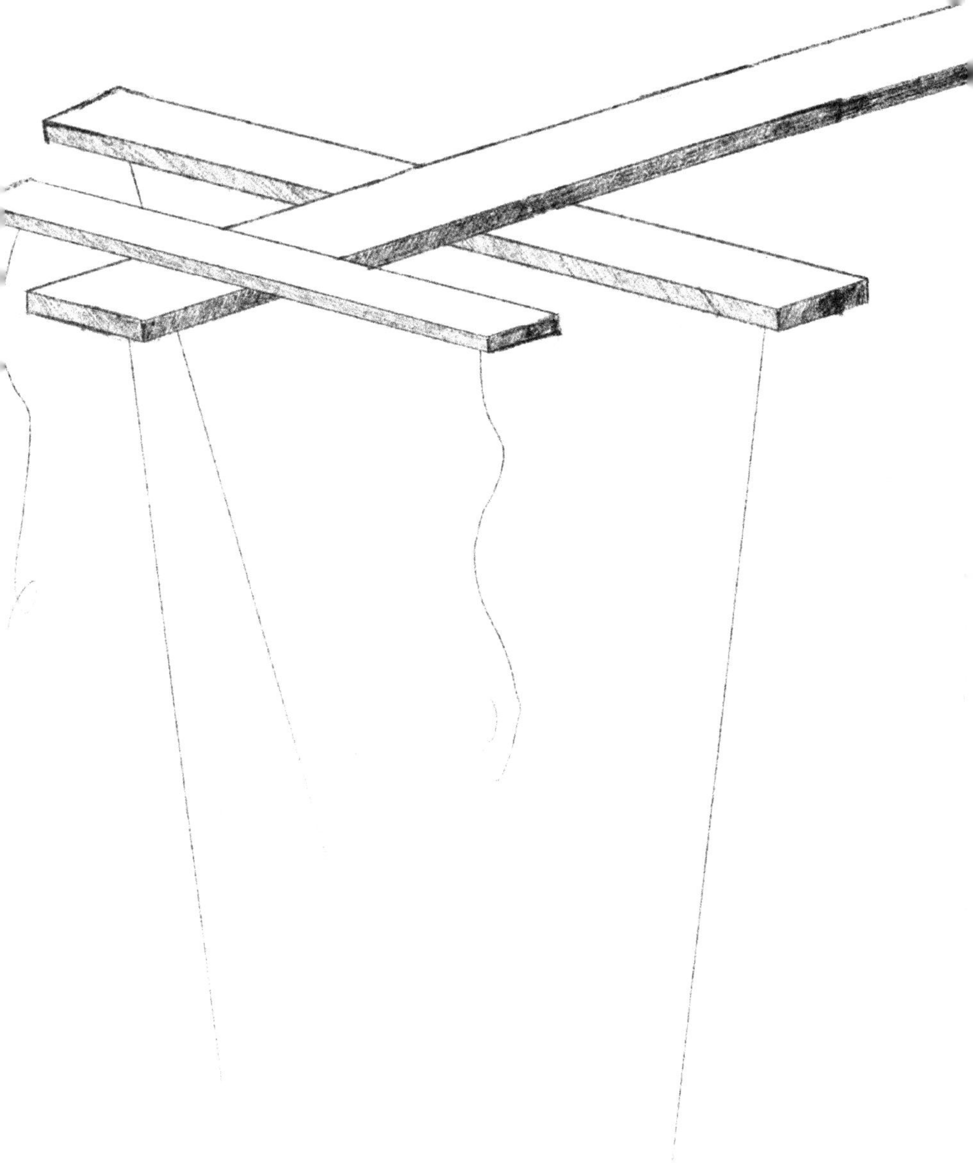

Wake up mind and say hello
For now it is time for you to put on a show
And show the way of where I need to be
Move my body intentionally
The vision of my life
and where it could be

-- The Puppeteer

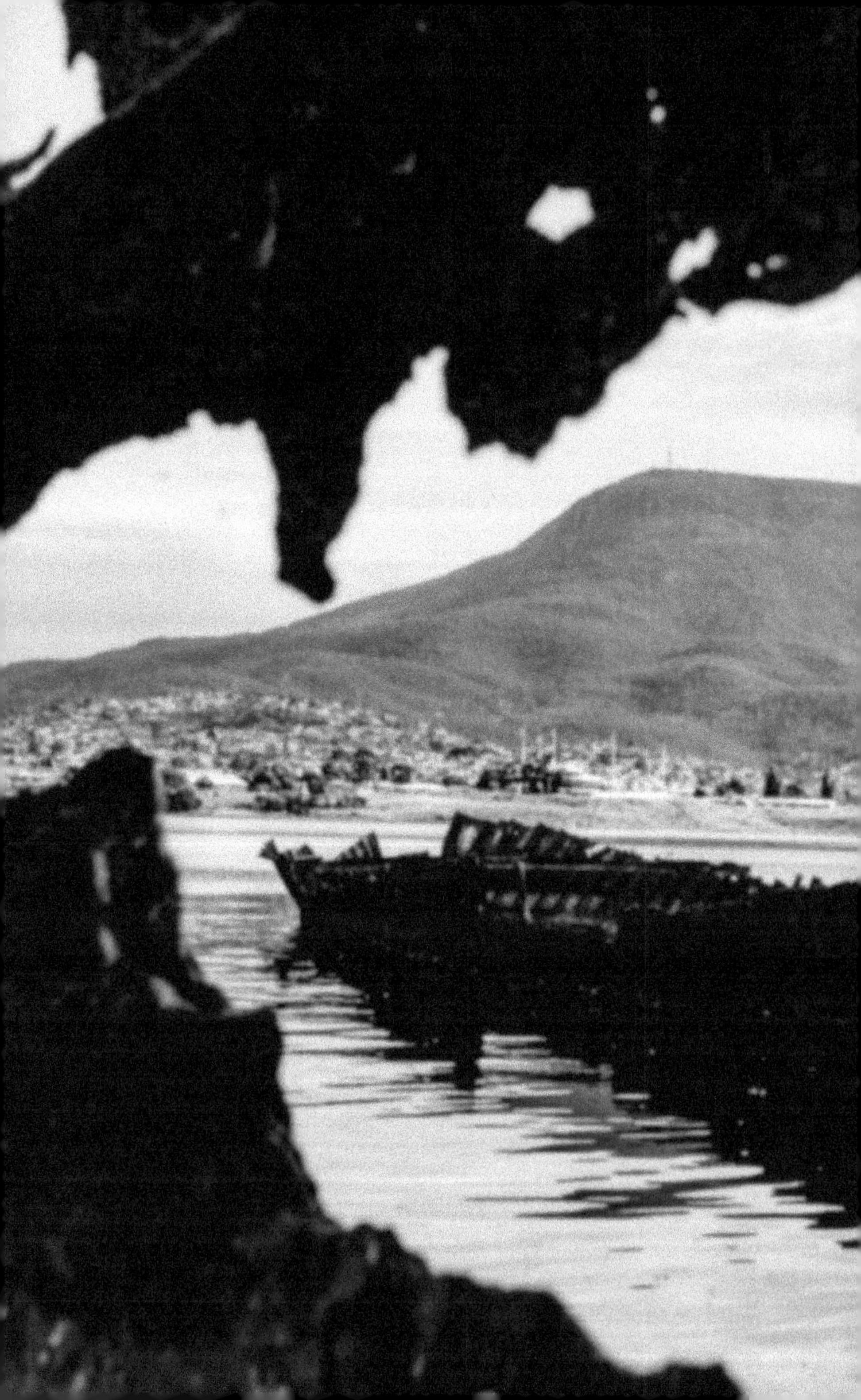

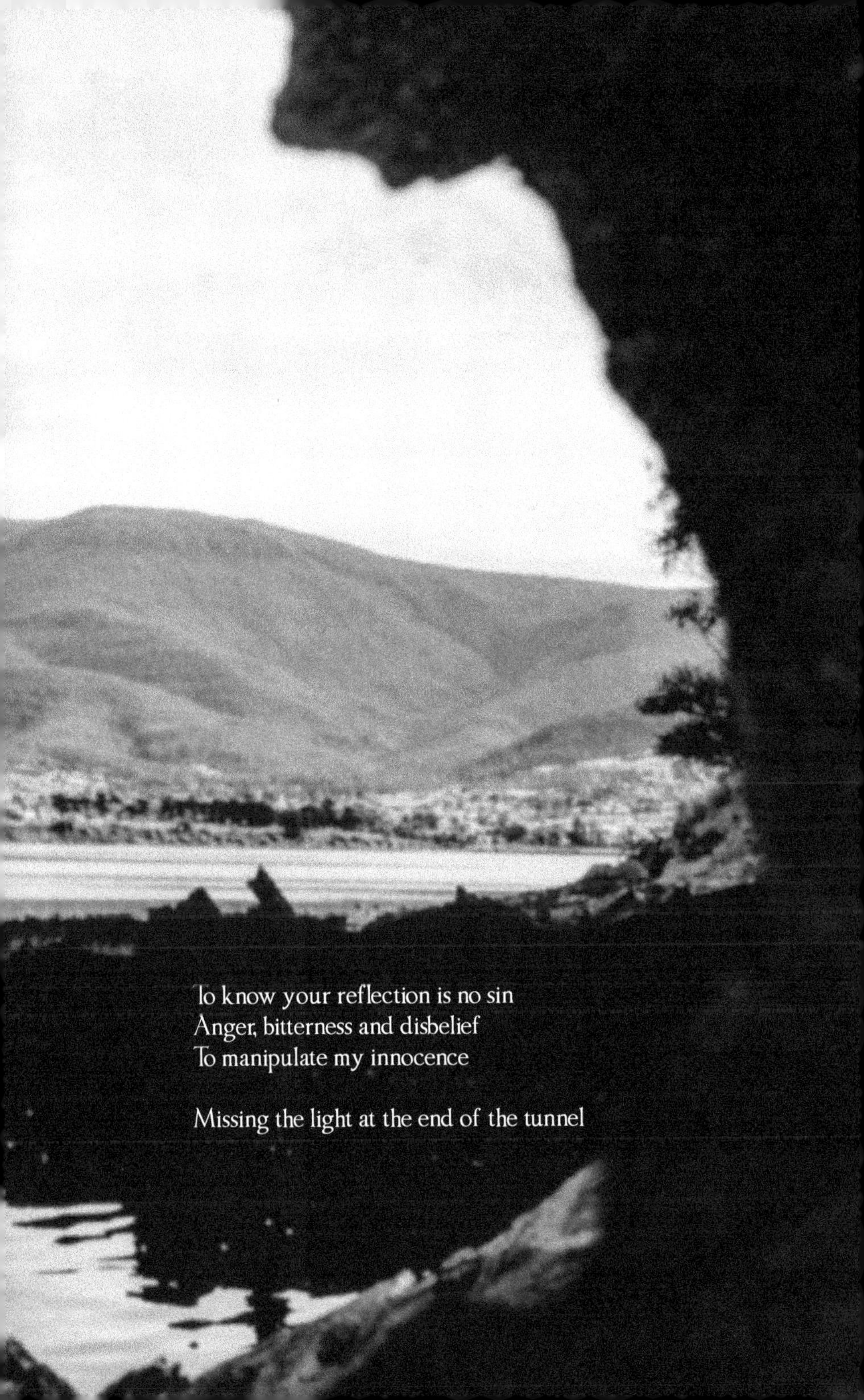

To know your reflection is no sin
Anger, bitterness and disbelief
To manipulate my innocence

Missing the light at the end of the tunnel

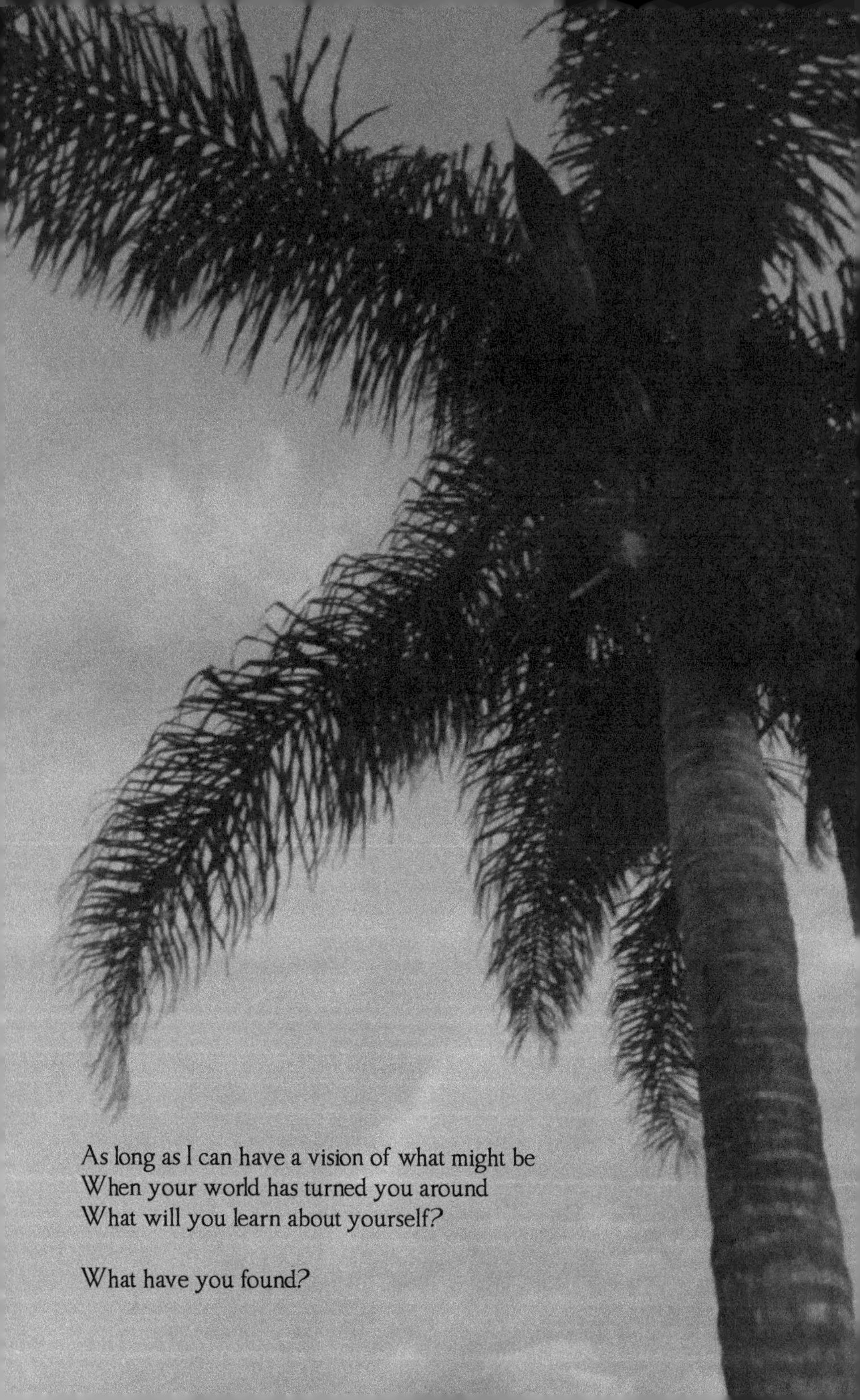

As long as I can have a vision of what might be
When your world has turned you around
What will you learn about yourself?

What have you found?

The phone rings
I don't answer it
Why is it that I just sit?

The sum of you is for all to see
The angel of light will set you free
The angel of light reminds you how strong you can be
The angel of light lets you completely see
To see the angel of light in all its glory
Makes for life's amazing story
To feel the light through the haze and the mist
The angel of light has one list
Caring,
Laughter,
Tenderness
And companionship unable to resist

Angel of light to guide me through
Outside the gates of hell
Angel of light walk with me
Angel of light make me all I can be.

-- Whispered in prayer

A spirit of a soul of whom you knew
Have they been drifting along with you?
You remember their laugh
Their love of life
To only have their life struck by one's sharp knife

They fought hard
And long
For what was dear
Even in the face of one's internal fear

A life for a life is what they say
Alas this will not happen today
Bitterness, revenge, nor redemption
Will bring him back

He rests forever in his family's stack
It is us that will begin to fill the hole
For a great loss of one who lived
A life full of spirit within his soul.

-- My world will not go blind

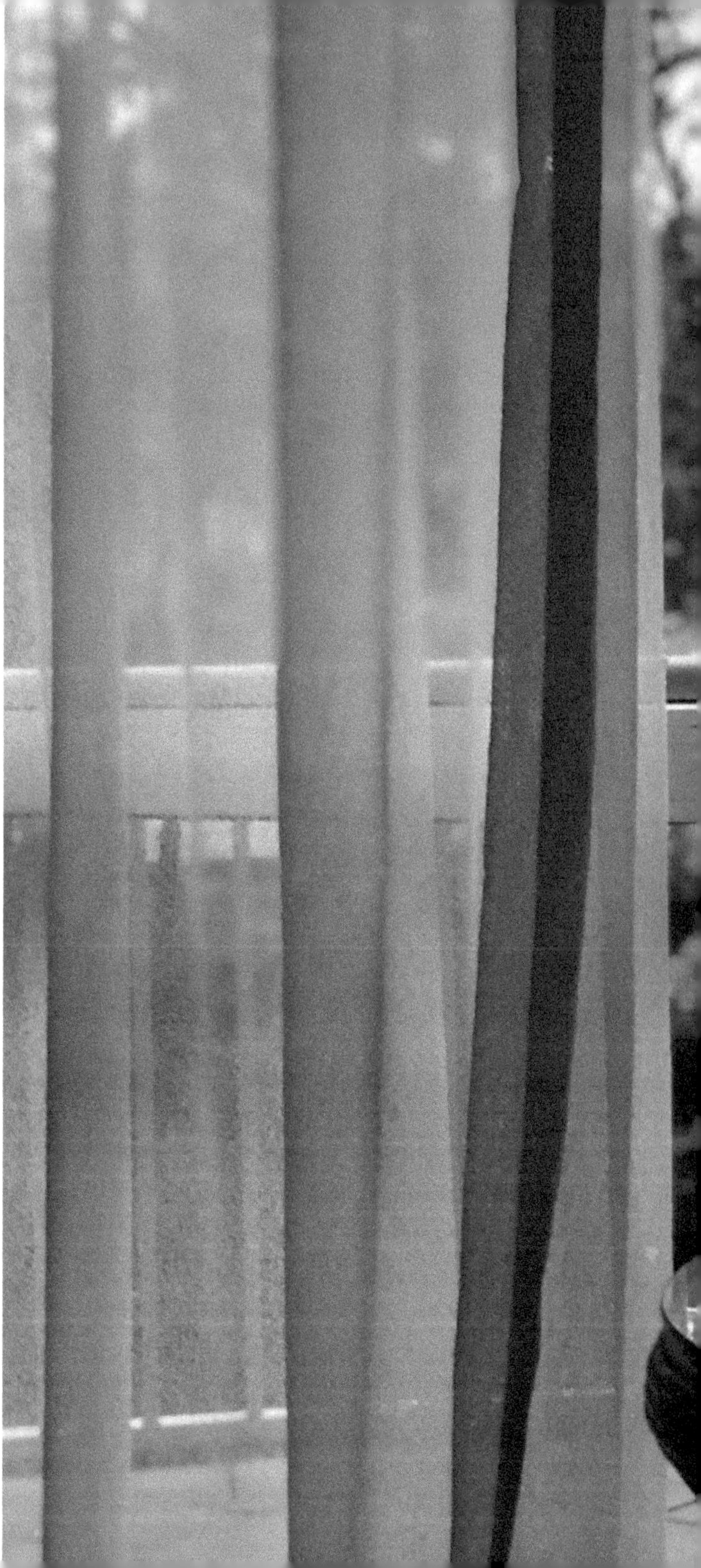

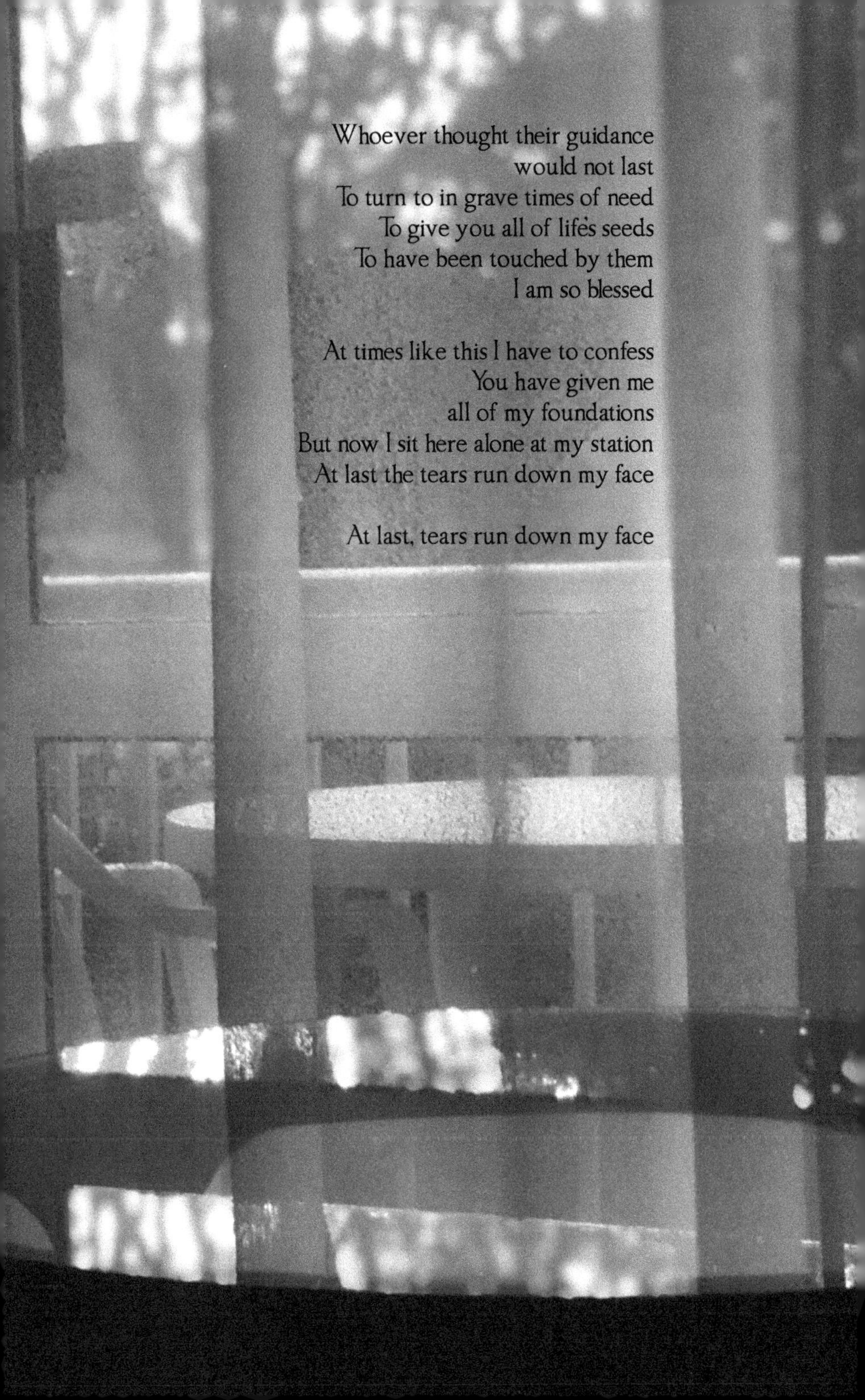

Whoever thought their guidance
would not last
To turn to in grave times of need
To give you all of life's seeds
To have been touched by them
I am so blessed

At times like this I have to confess
You have given me
all of my foundations
But now I sit here alone at my station
At last the tears run down my face

At last, tears run down my face

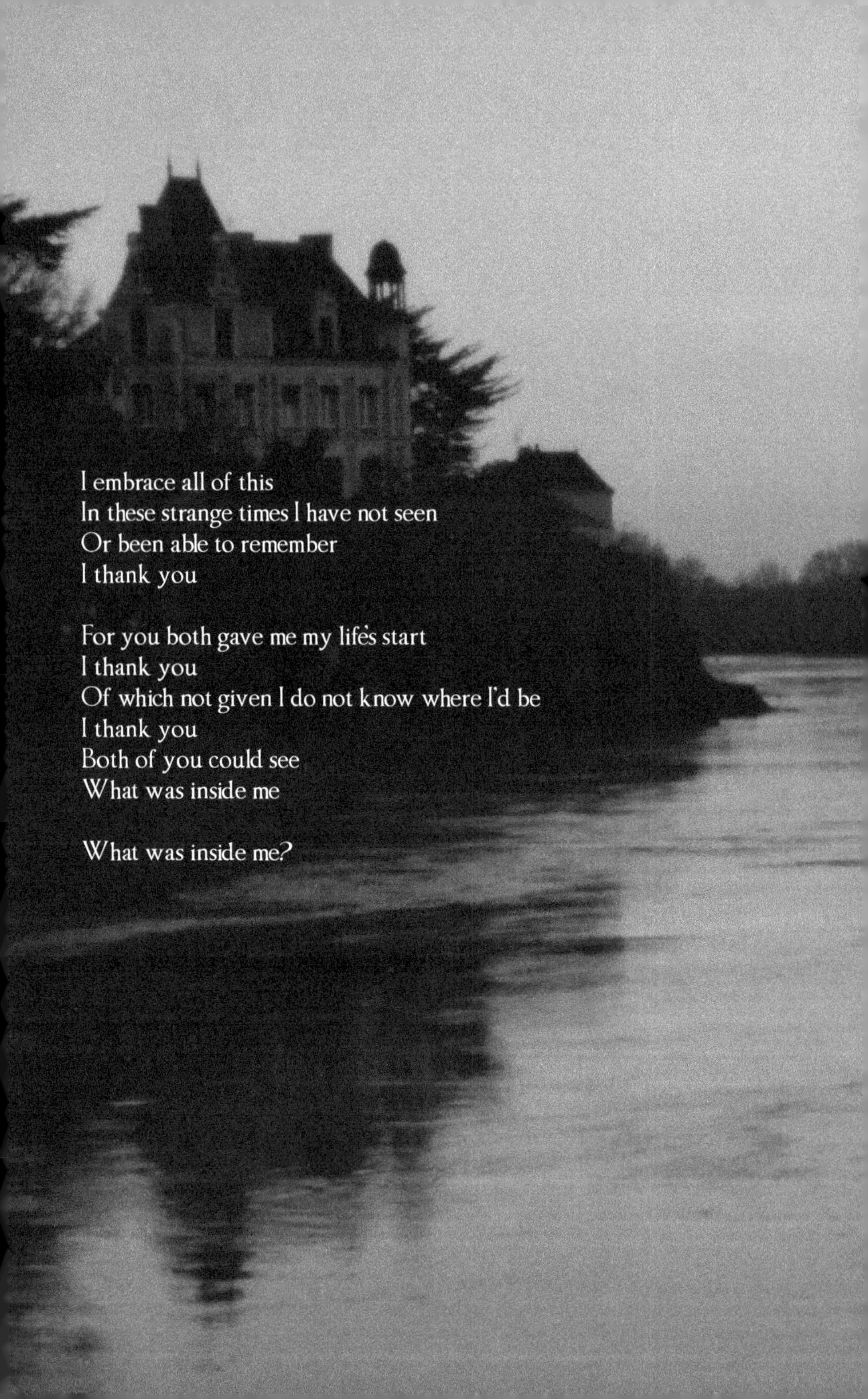

I embrace all of this
In these strange times I have not seen
Or been able to remember
I thank you

For you both gave me my life's start
I thank you
Of which not given I do not know where I'd be
I thank you
Both of you could see
What was inside me

What was inside me?

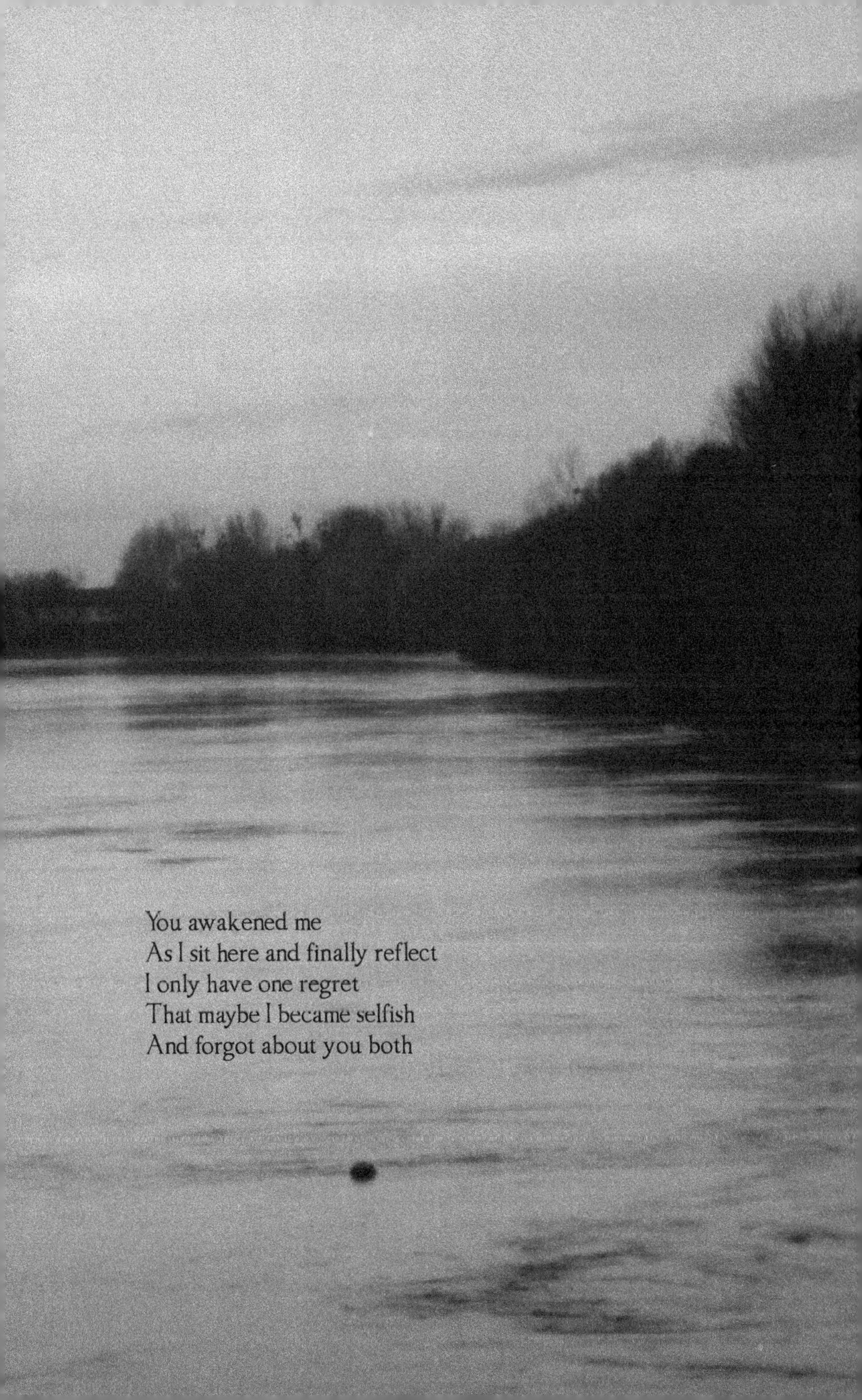

You awakened me
As I sit here and finally reflect
I only have one regret
That maybe I became selfish
And forgot about you both

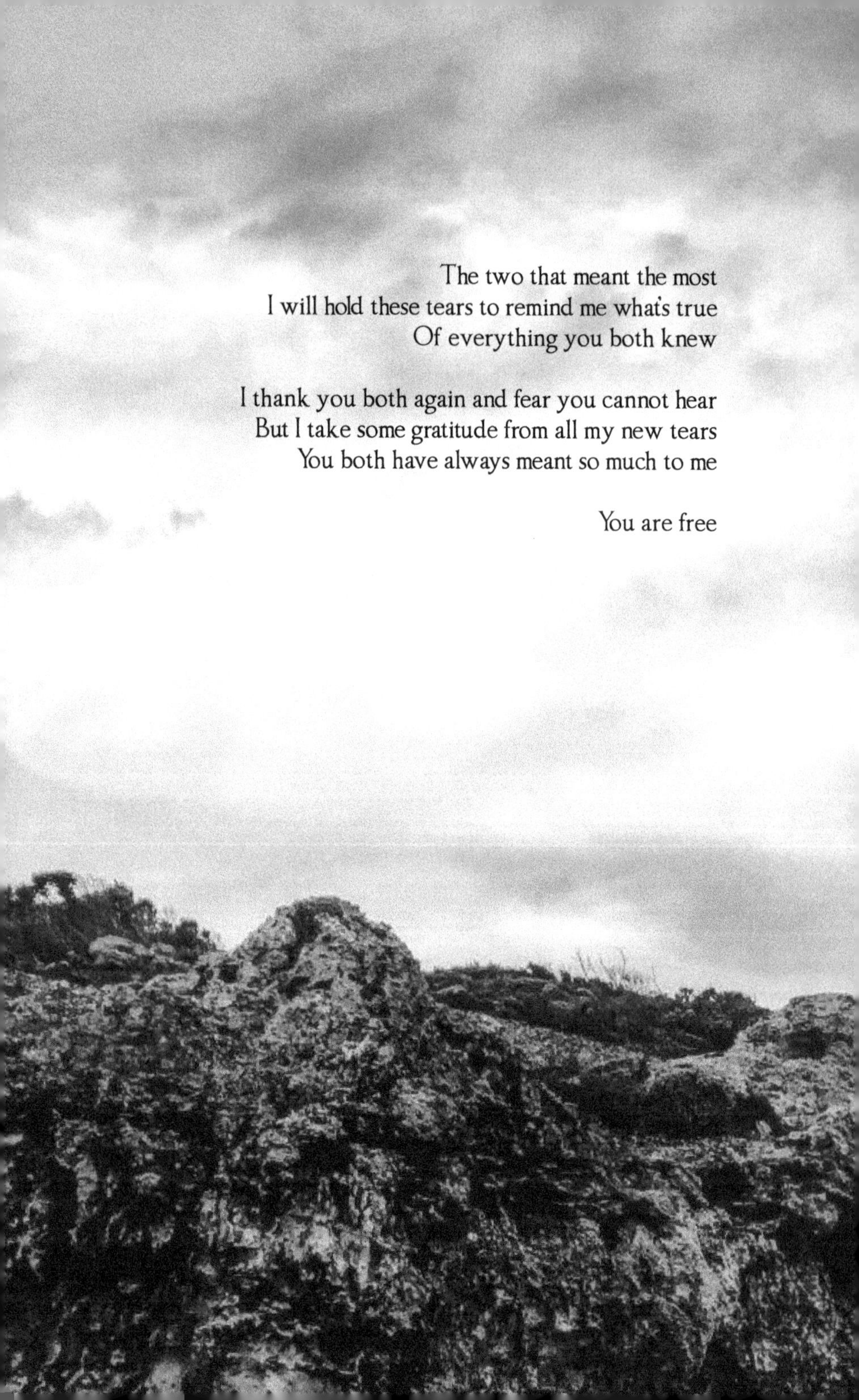

The two that meant the most
I will hold these tears to remind me what's true
Of everything you both knew

I thank you both again and fear you cannot hear
But I take some gratitude from all my new tears
You both have always meant so much to me

You are free

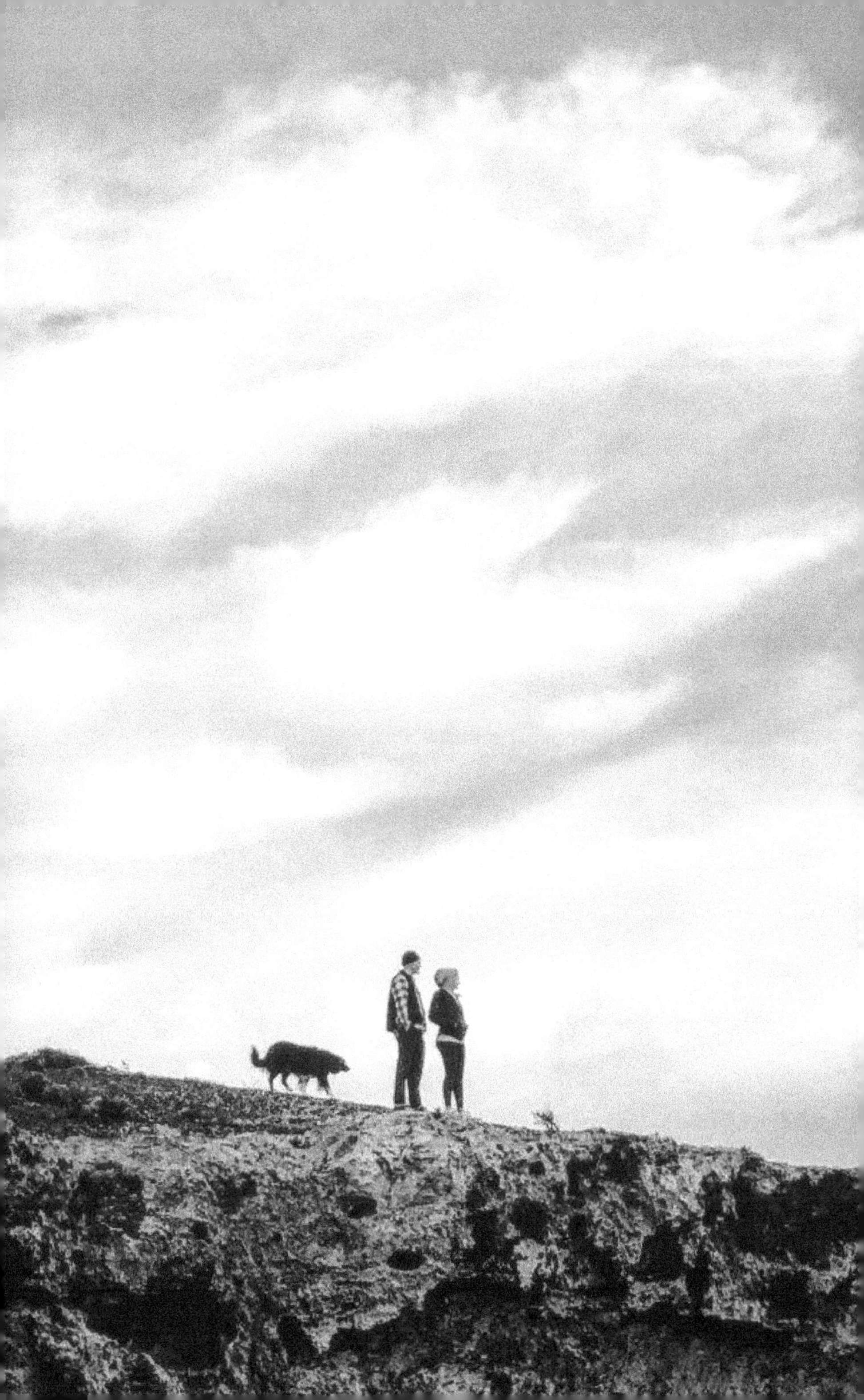

To remember is not a crime

Grief is not a punishment

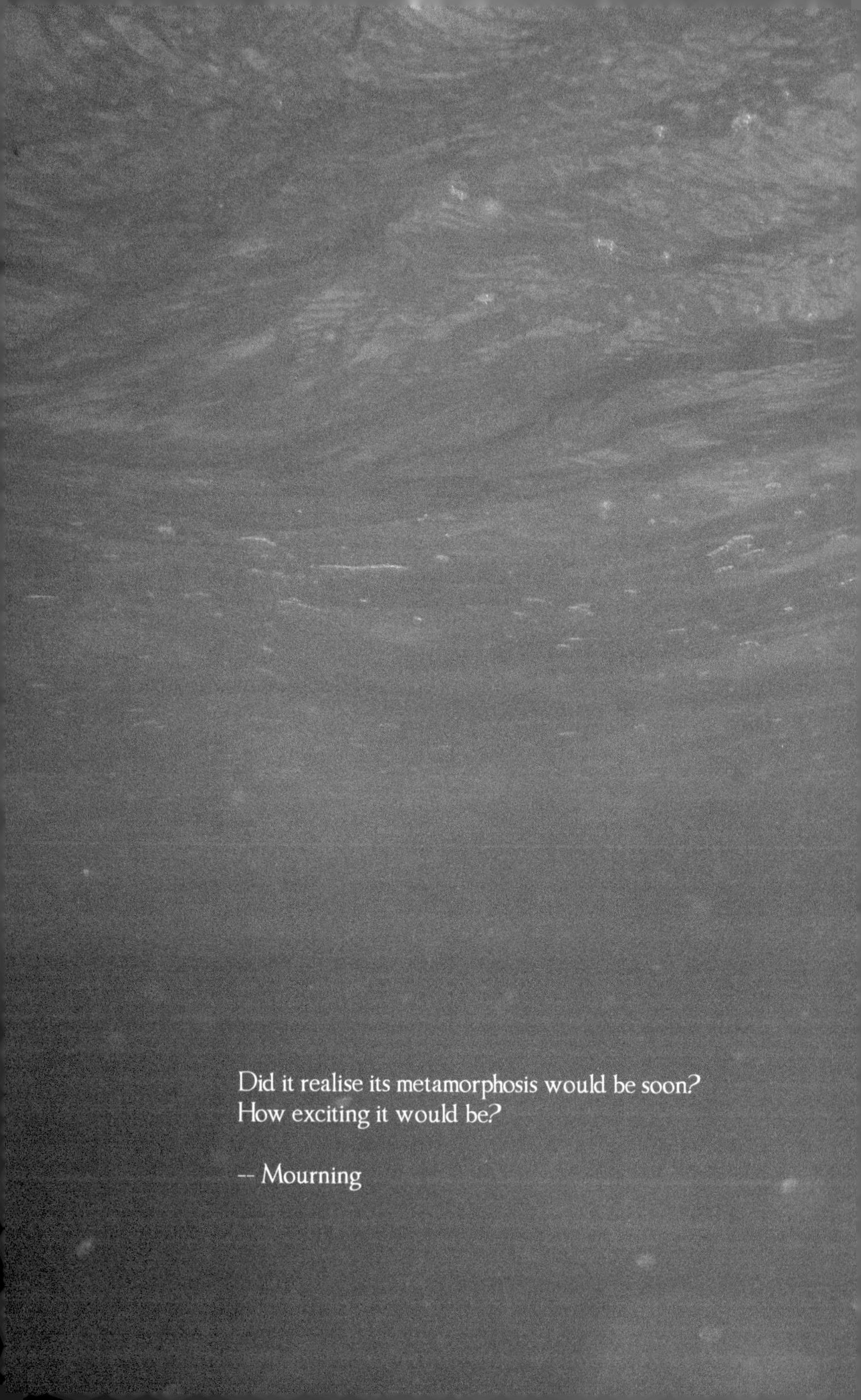

Did it realise its metamorphosis would be soon?
How exciting it would be?

-- Mourning

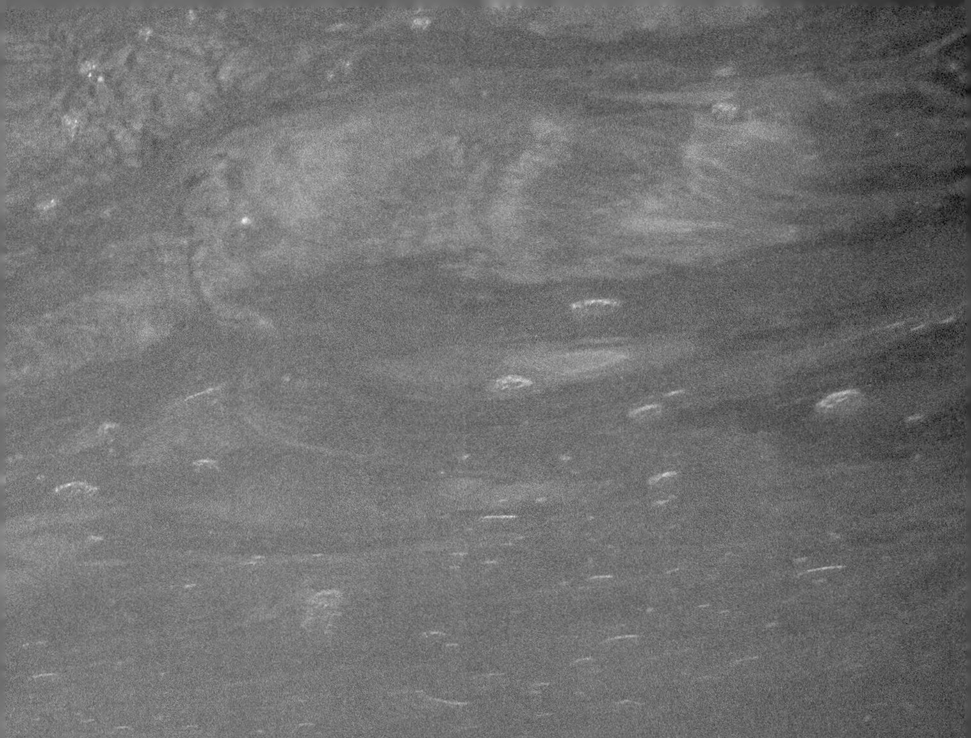

Show me
Show me how to be
Show me how you knew me

I pause to see you pass me by
You seem to soar so high
I am happy you are set free

You can finally see
Enjoy your time with the sky
And may you always be able to fly.

-- Show me

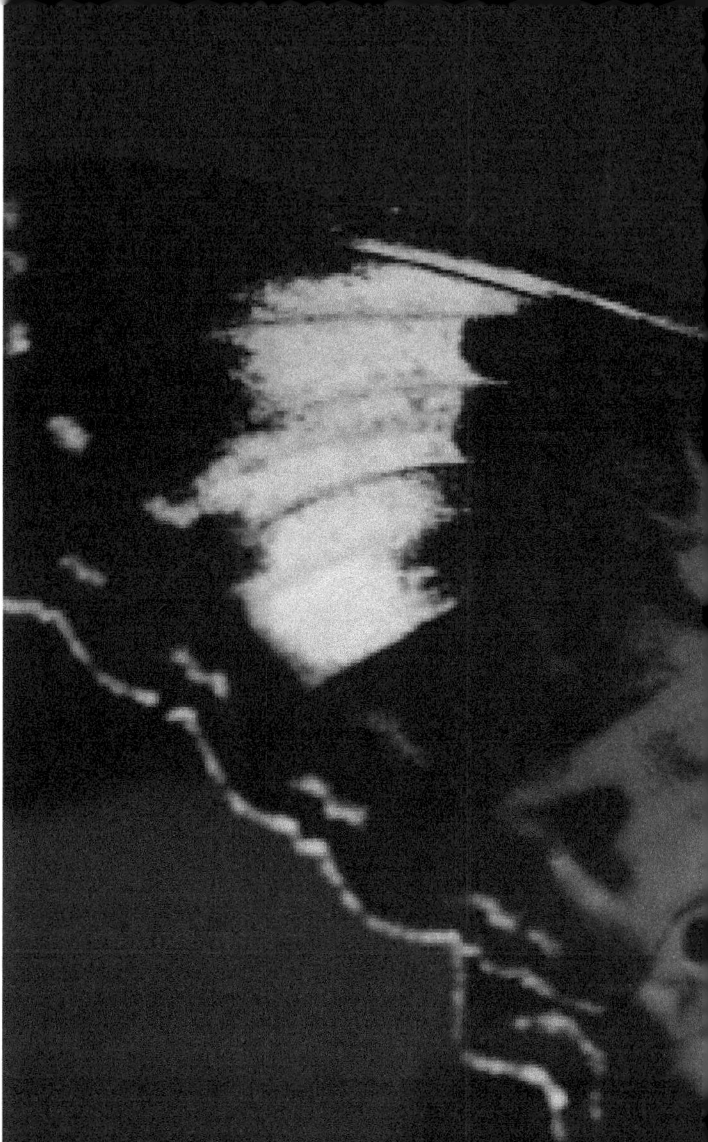

When it awakes and sees
The opportunities in front of it
Will it pause and sit
Or allow its natural flight to play
Who really knows what it might say
It is an amazing sight to see
When this butterfly sets itself free

– Spreading wings

Arise from your cocoon slumber
For Father Time knows your number
How do you know to take flight?
What do you see in your sight?

— The Butterfly

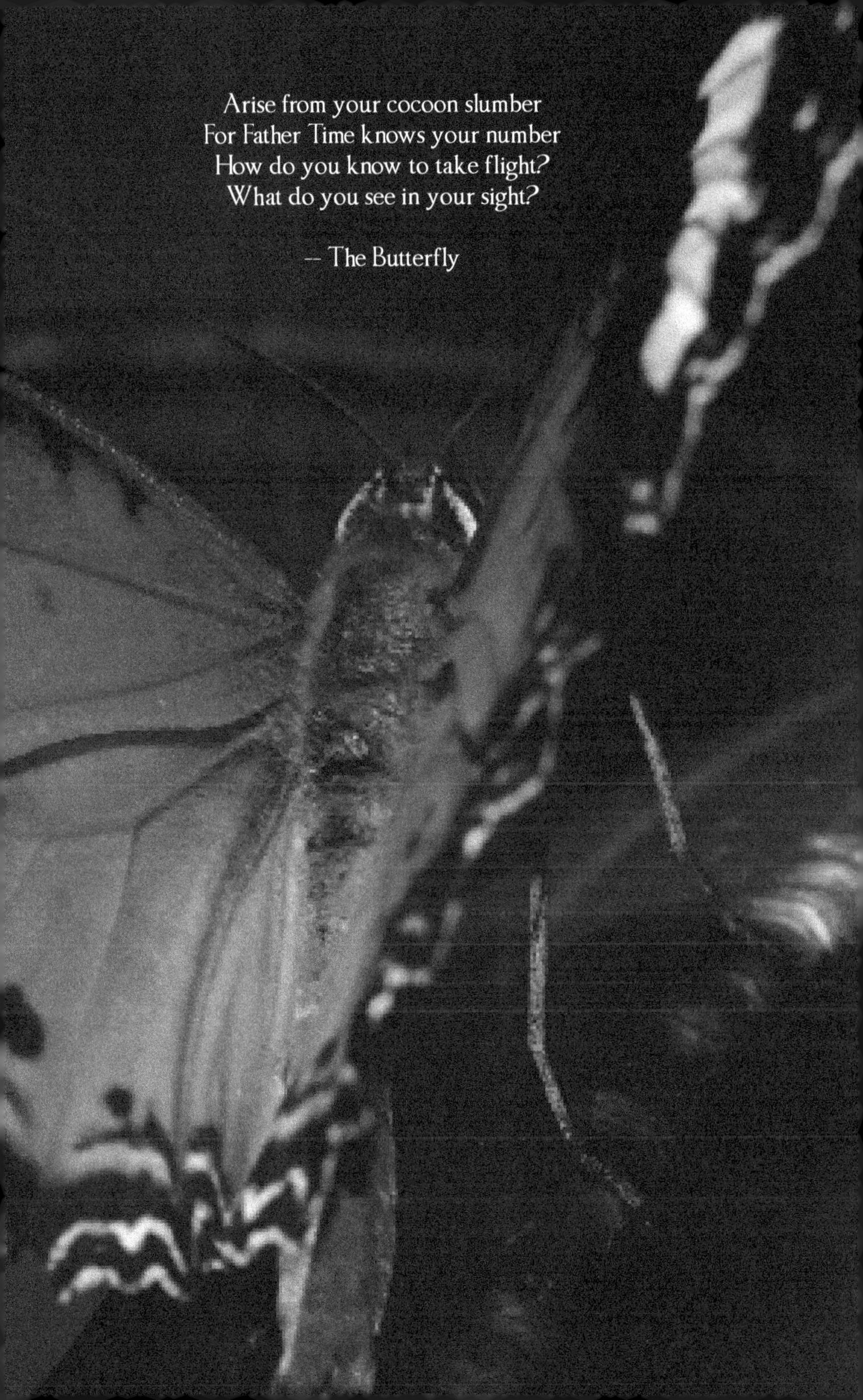

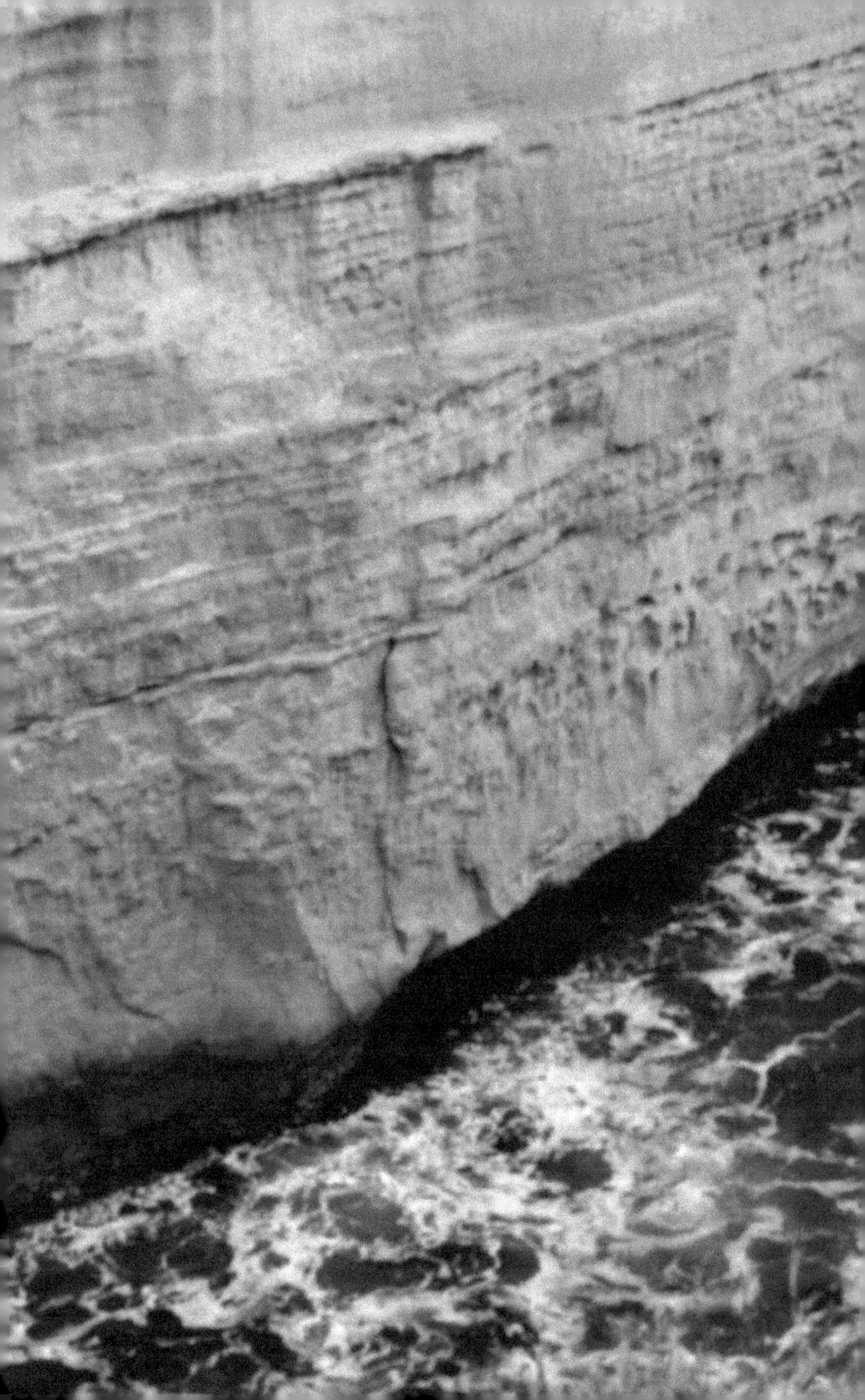

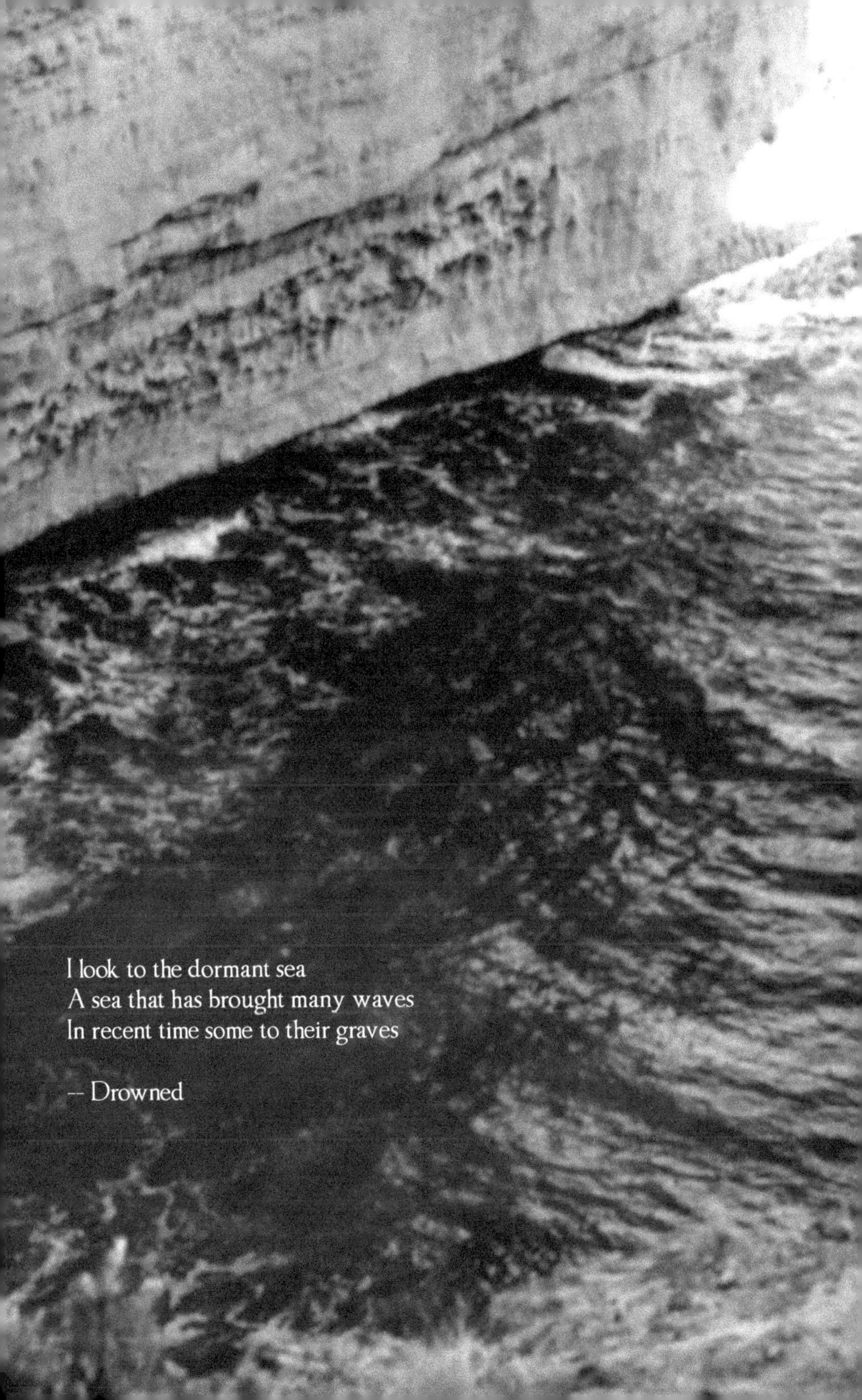

I look to the dormant sea
A sea that has brought many waves
In recent time some to their graves

— Drowned

Only for my eyes to see
Juggling the emotions that will be
And balancing the want to be free
When I die what will they say?

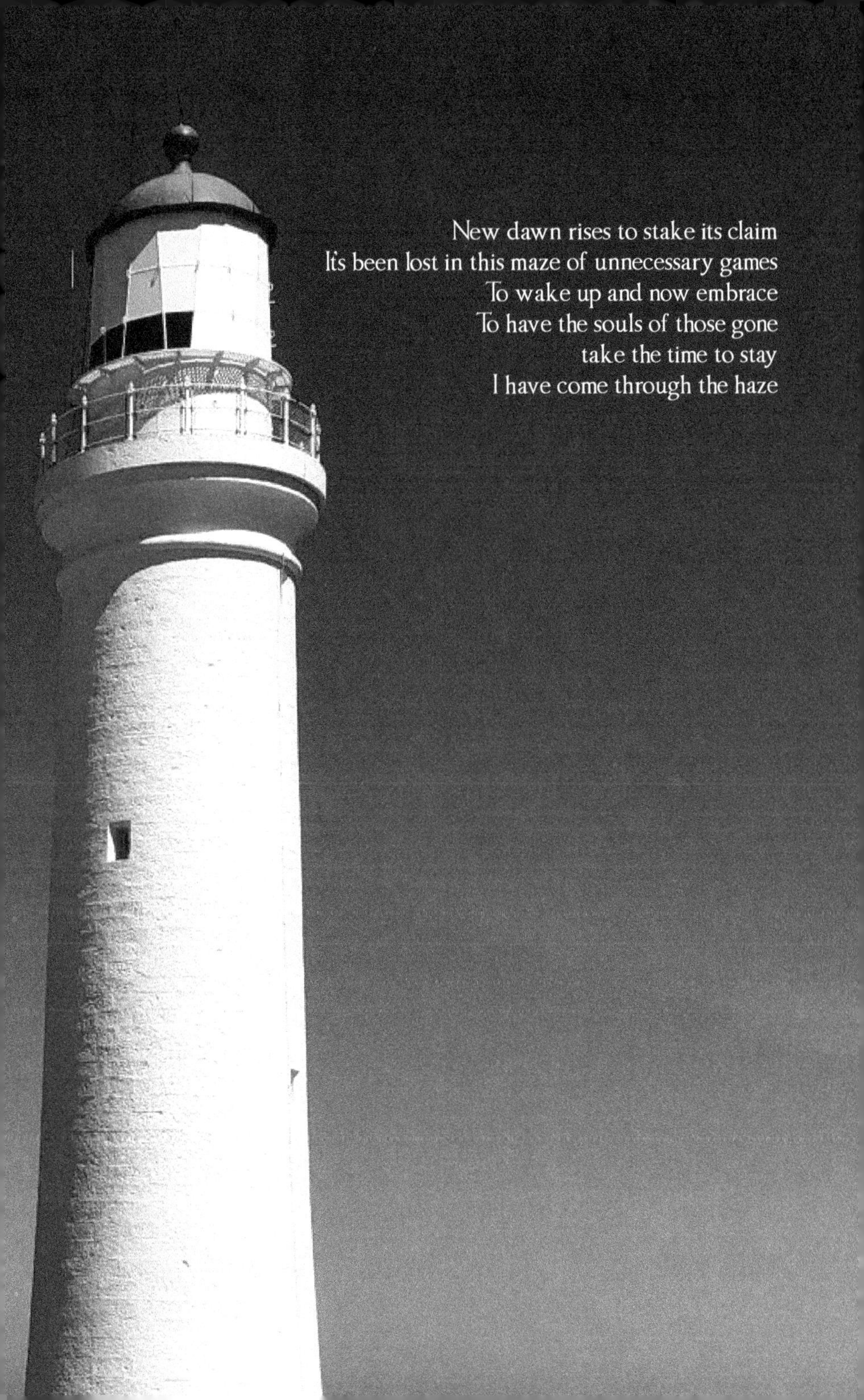

New dawn rises to stake its claim
It's been lost in this maze of unnecessary games
To wake up and now embrace
To have the souls of those gone
take the time to stay
I have come through the haze

From this pause I see.
I just may find
By embracing my daily grind
The weather right now is clear

-- Compass

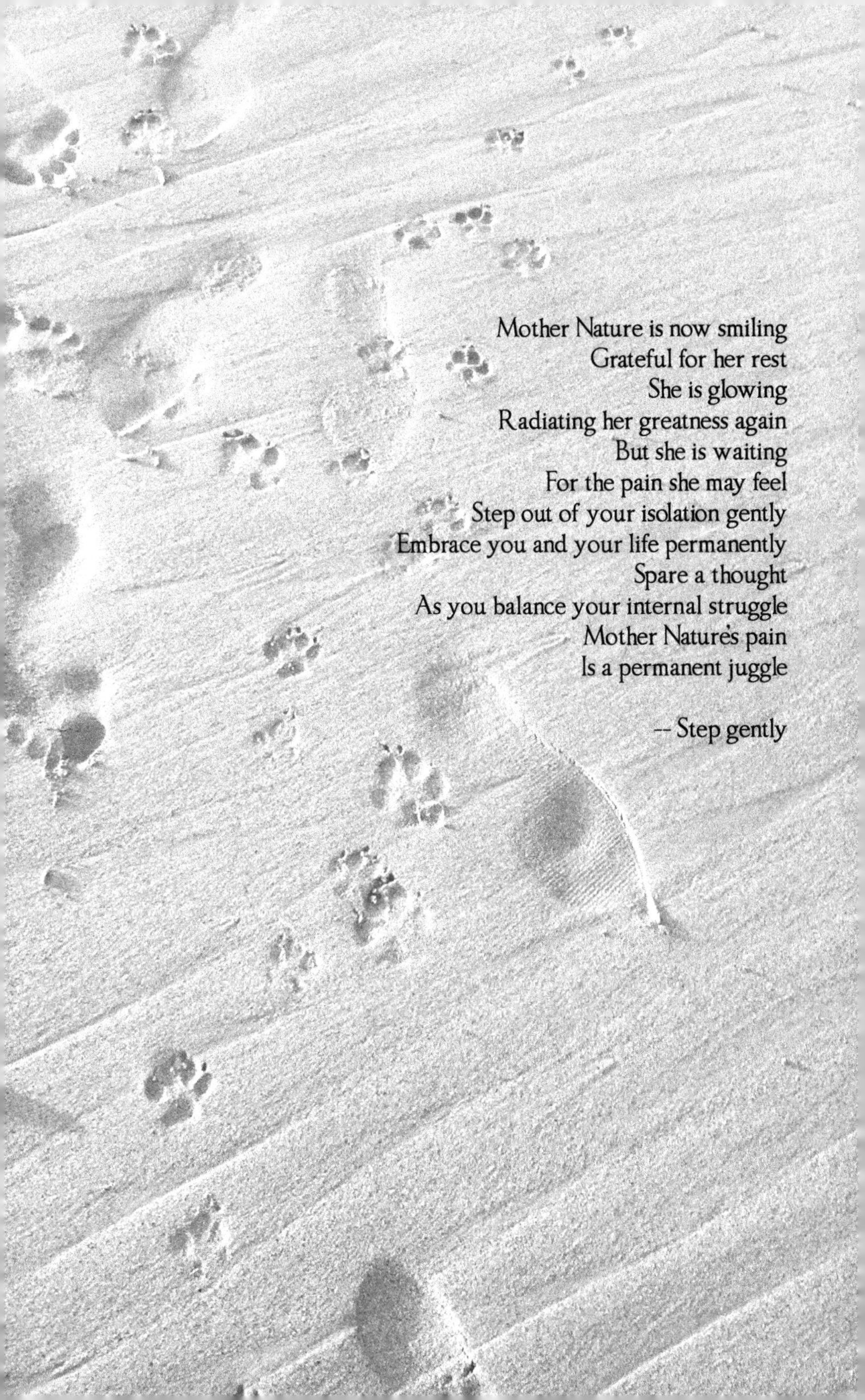

Mother Nature is now smiling
Grateful for her rest
She is glowing
Radiating her greatness again
But she is waiting
For the pain she may feel
Step out of your isolation gently
Embrace you and your life permanently
Spare a thought
As you balance your internal struggle
Mother Nature's pain
Is a permanent juggle

-- Step gently

For the sum of me
Allows me to be unique
The part of me that remains
I will always keep

-- The art of letting go

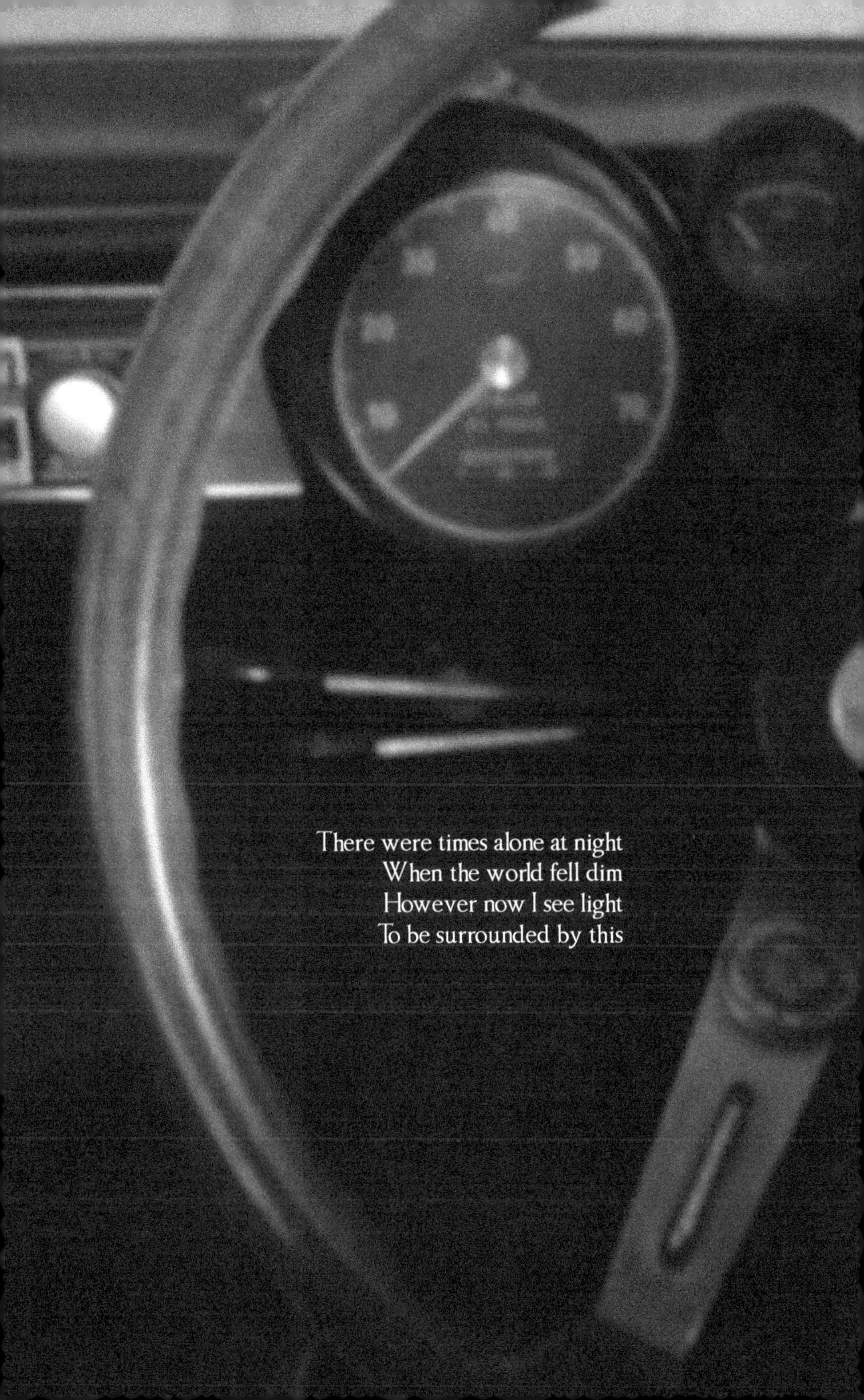

There were times alone at night
When the world fell dim
However now I see light
To be surrounded by this

I don't have much
But what I am
is built within

-- Home.

It is not me I see
When I walk in the carpark at night
It is there where I see lonely sights
When I sit alone
When I walk along the street
Is this a state of mind?
When you venture into your darkest internal fight
It is here where you need to dance within life's light
For if you always see lonely sights
So awake and embrace all that is near
And walk into the corridor of fear

-- Learning to walk alone

I hope.
As I build again
I hope.

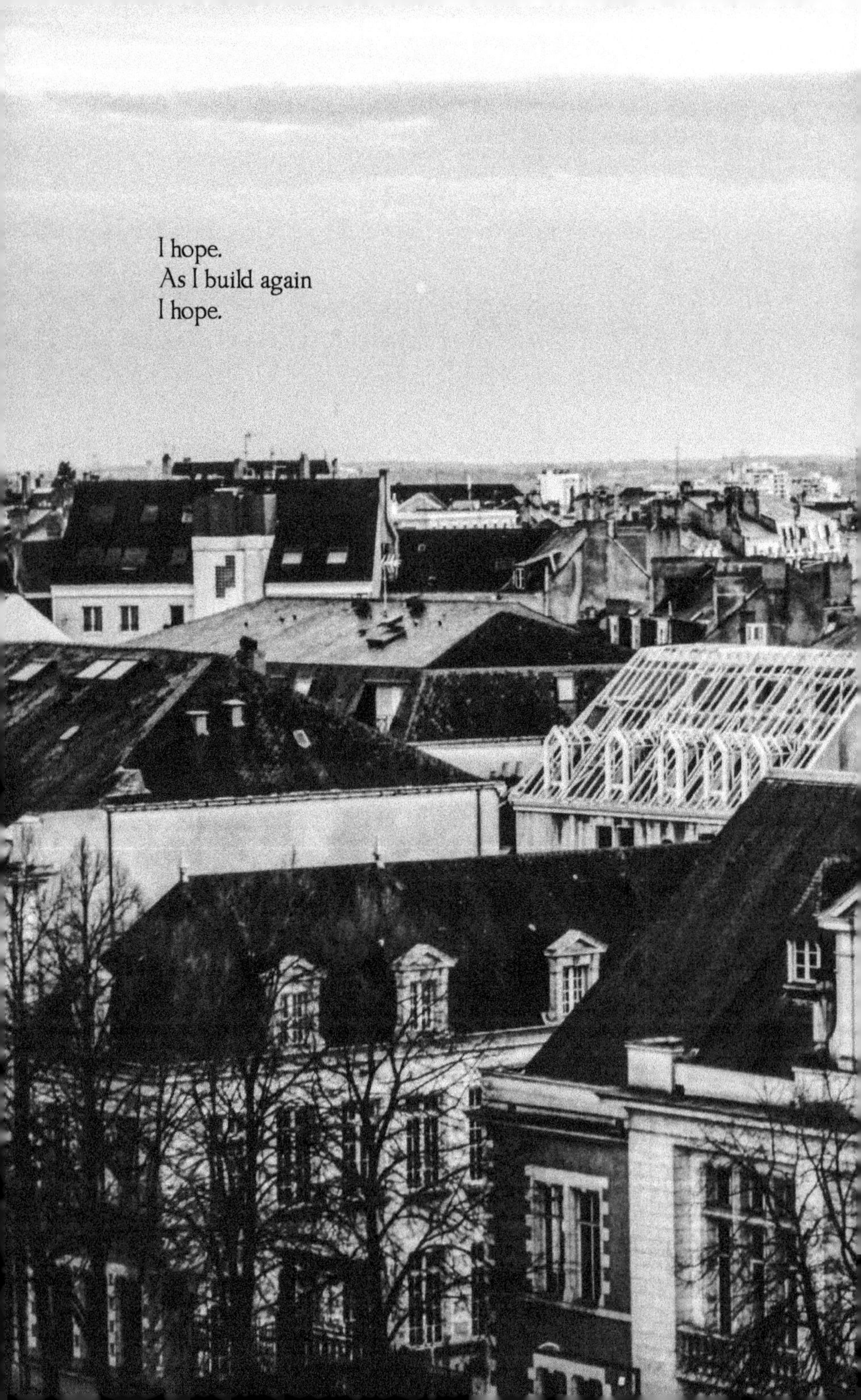

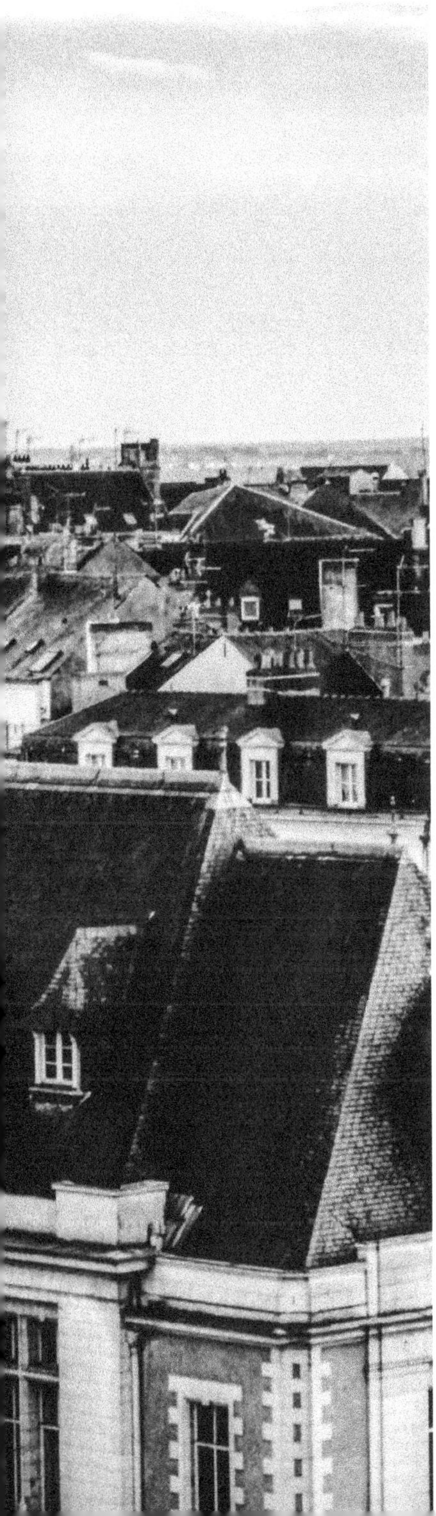

It's your eyes
That have awakened me
Those passionate eyes
Now set free

Connecting my insides
By walking by your side
For the beauty I see

-- U the human set free

Look from my reflective eyes

I will not tell myself to hide

I am still whole without you

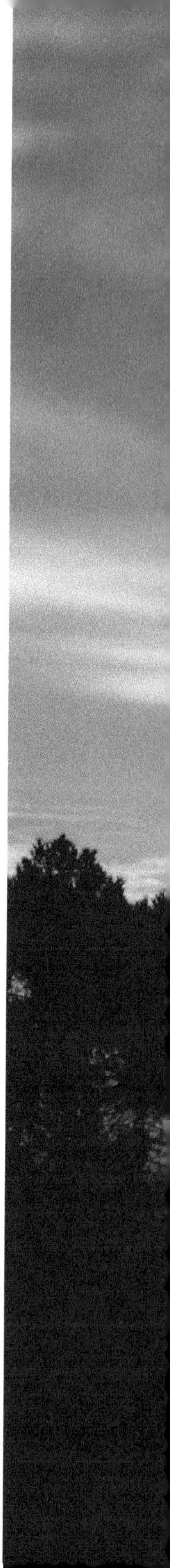

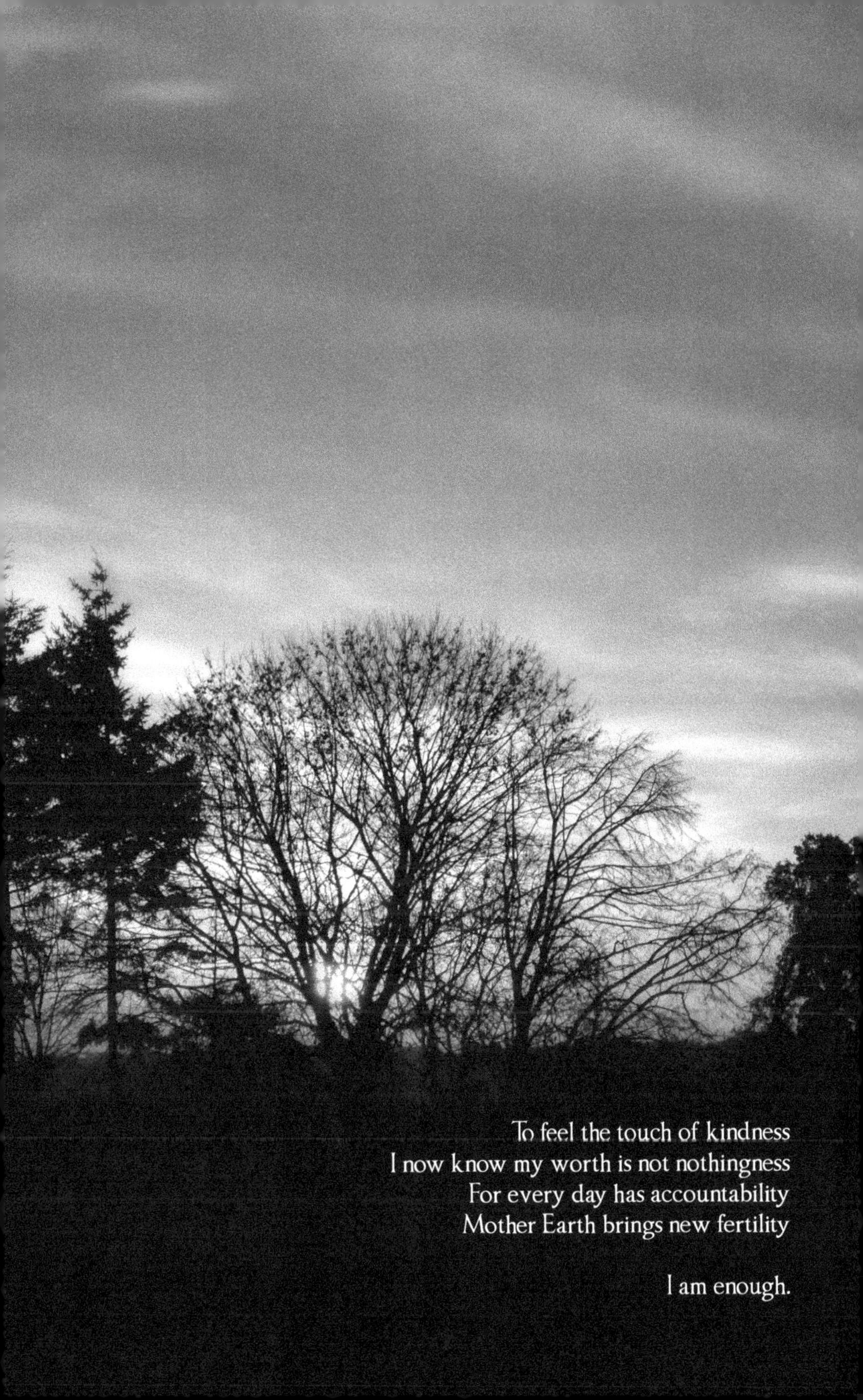

To feel the touch of kindness
I now know my worth is not nothingness
For every day has accountability
Mother Earth brings new fertility

I am enough.

Will you ever know
What it is like to grow
As I walk out the door
Not able to give anymore
I feel the sadness of time
Disappointed of not seeing the signs
I will be who I'll be

-- Comfortable within myself

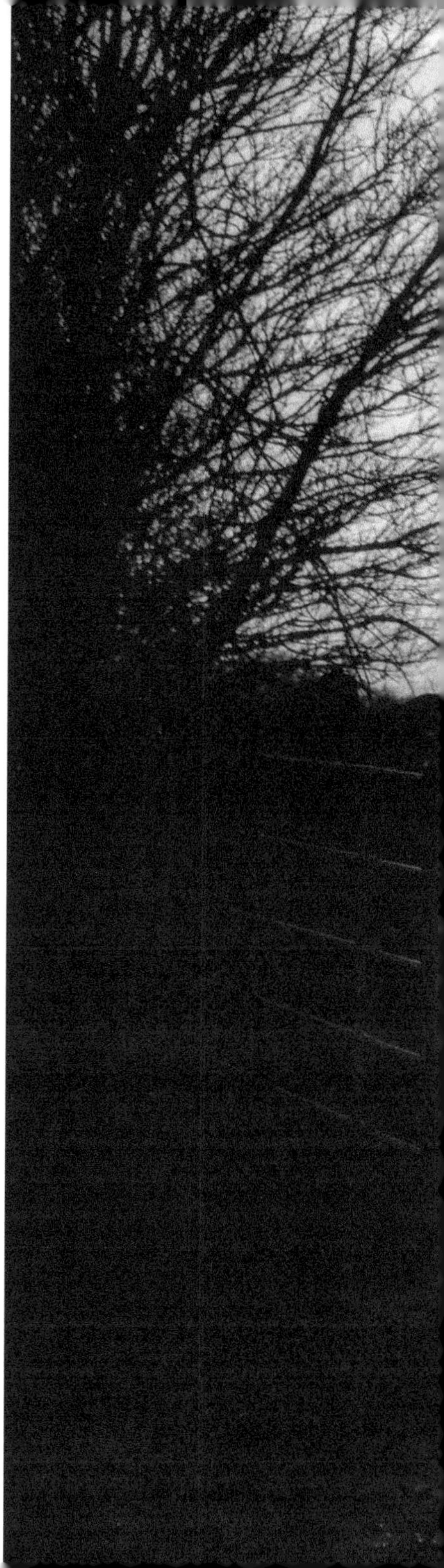

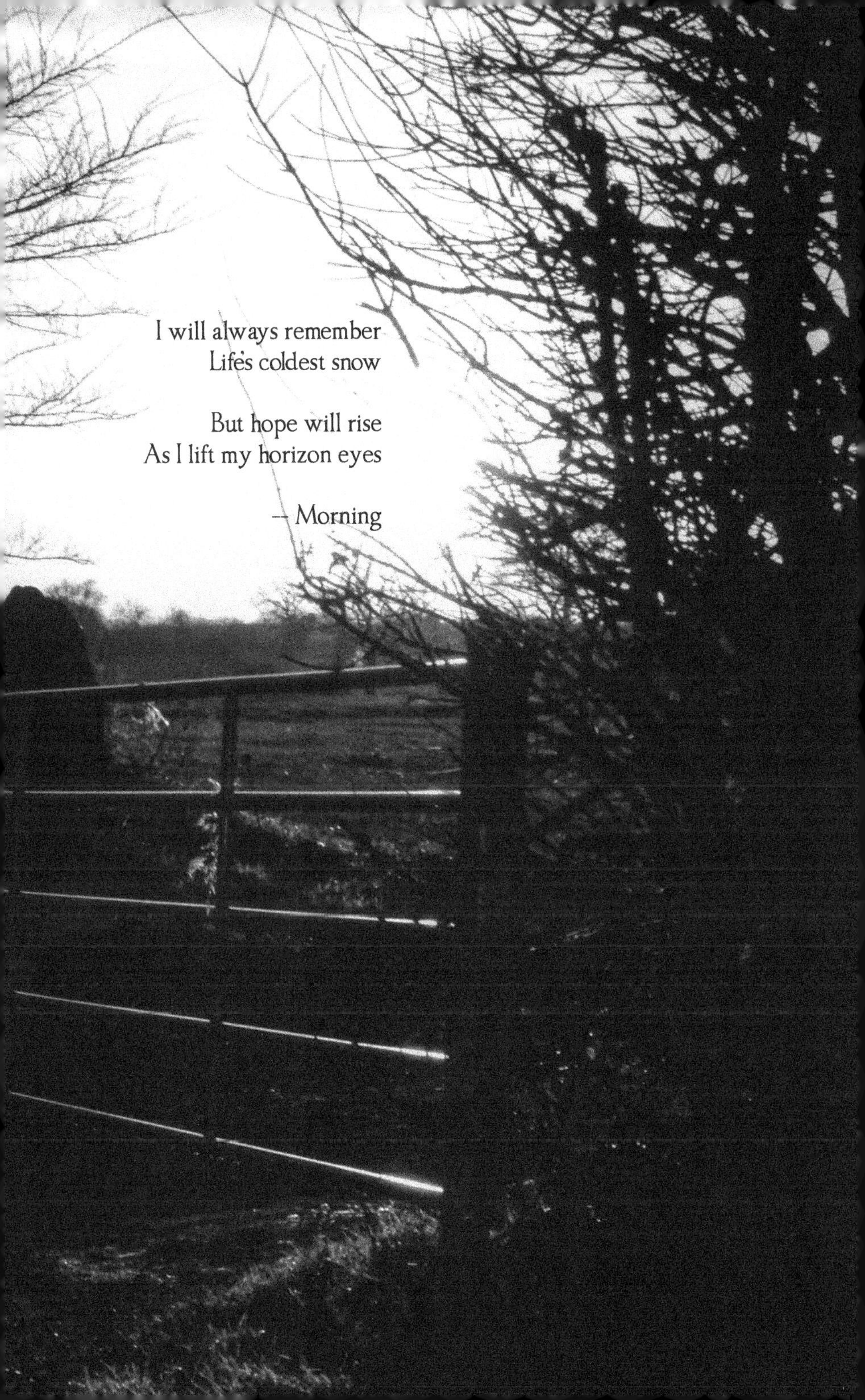

I will always remember
Life's coldest snow

But hope will rise
As I lift my horizon eyes

-- Morning

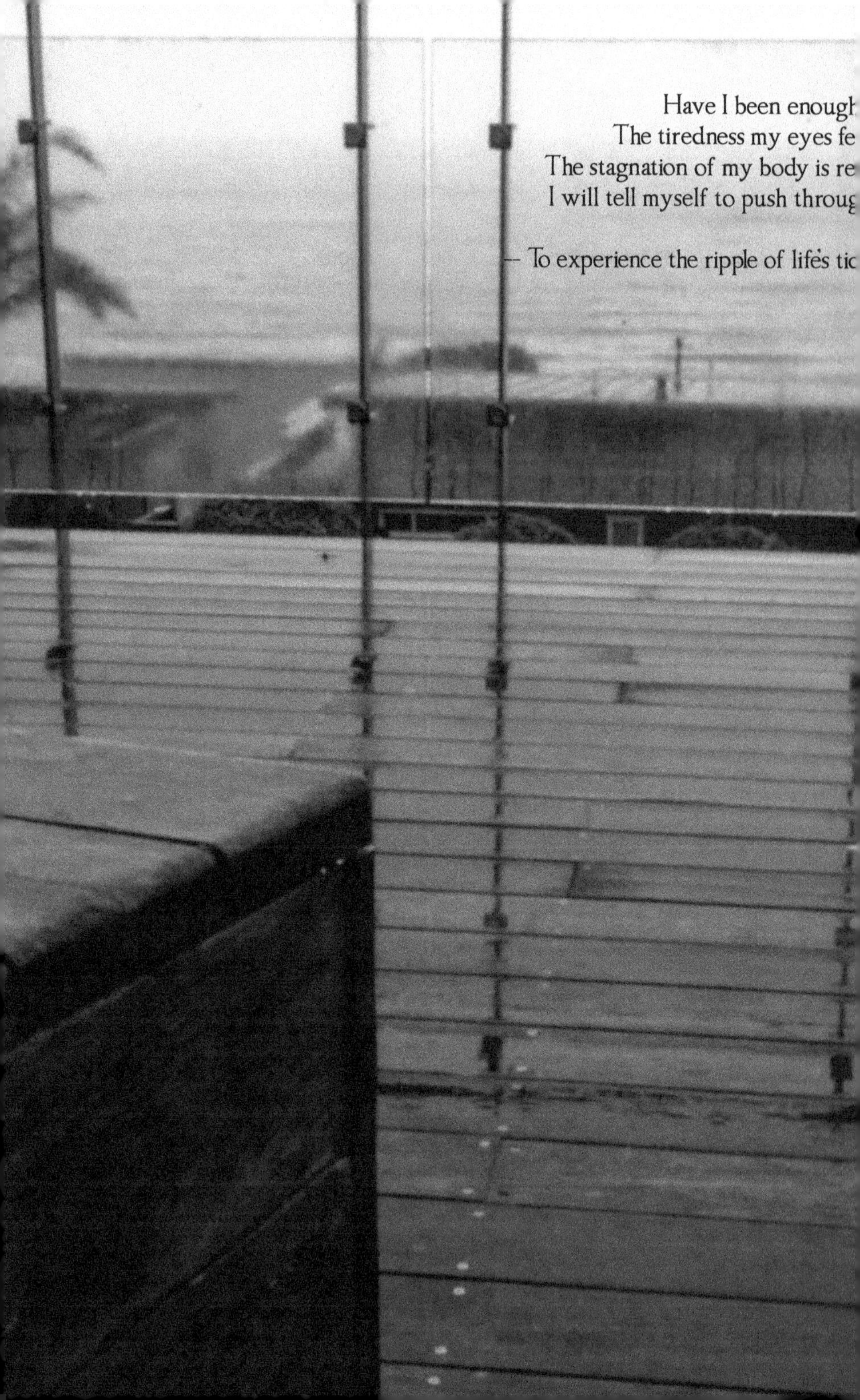

Have I been enoug
The tiredness my eyes fe
The stagnation of my body is re
I will tell myself to push throug

— To experience the ripple of life's tic

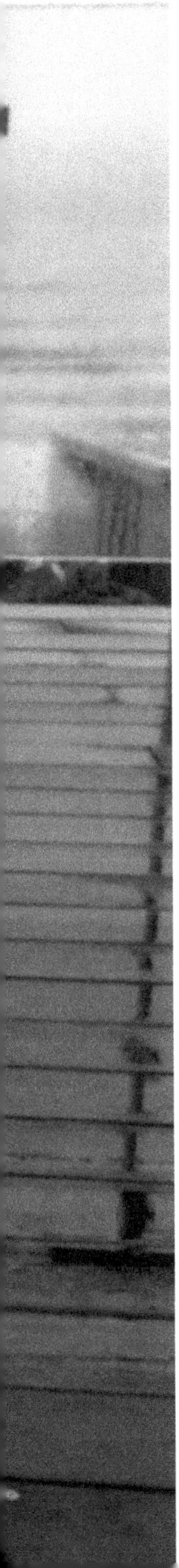

Who sees life's light from a different lens
One that can't be held within conforming pens
For feel the life when your mind is free
And embrace your happiness for what it will be.

-- I pen my letters with a quill

For what is love and what will it be
It begins internally
Live in your reflection
Await at your pond for your connection

– To wait or run

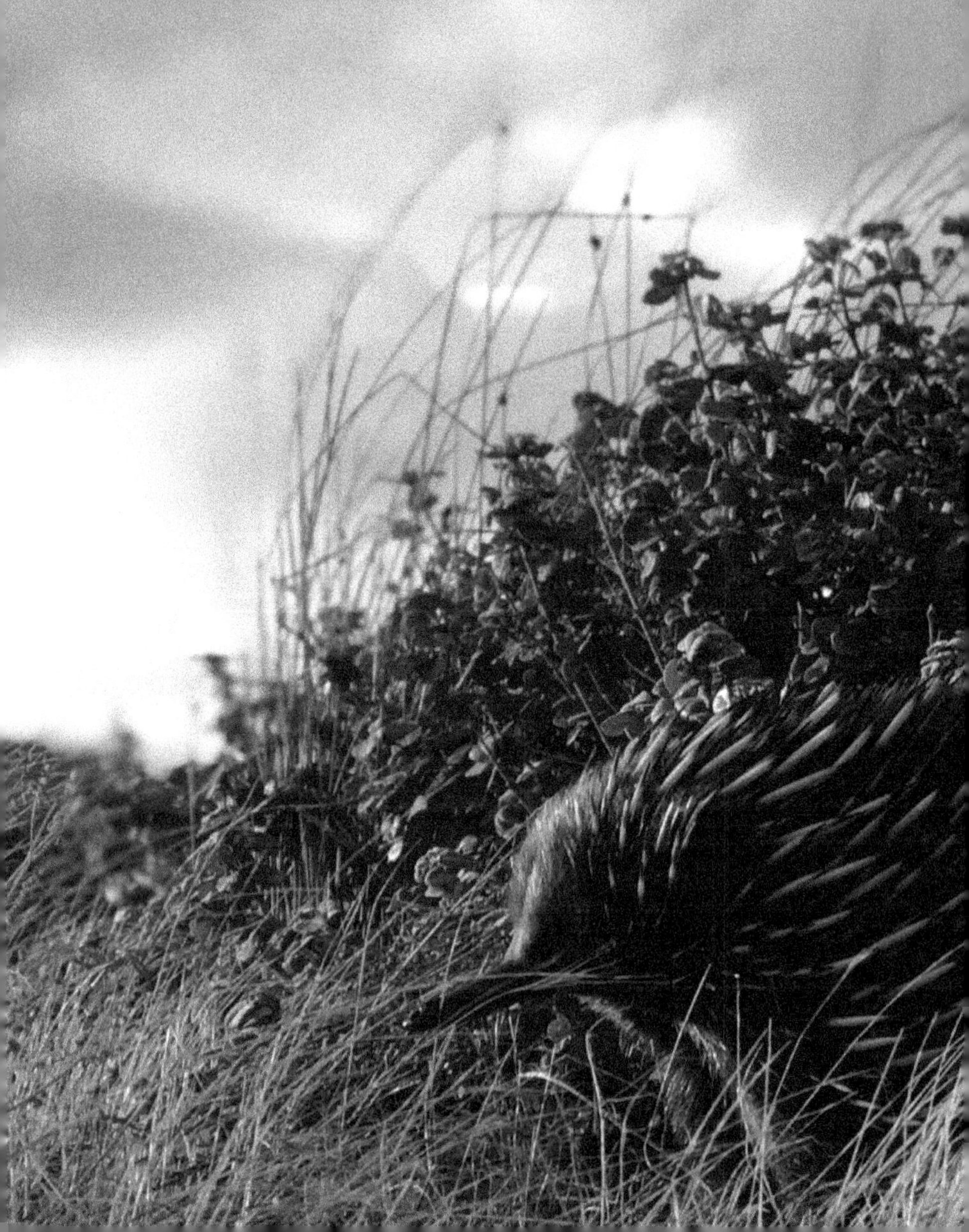

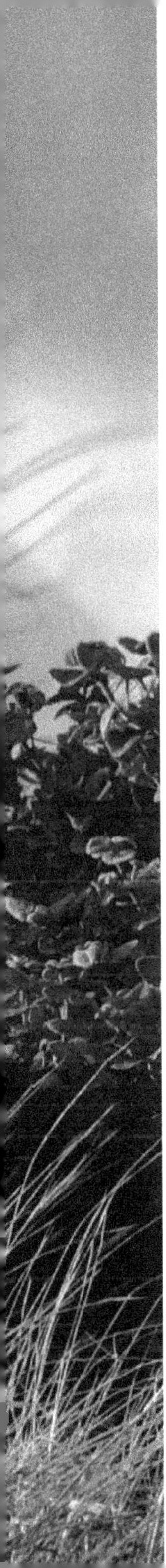

Now be kind to yourself and let your mind be free
Of all of the harshness you ultimately see
Arise again and be proud of you

For you are one of the chosen few

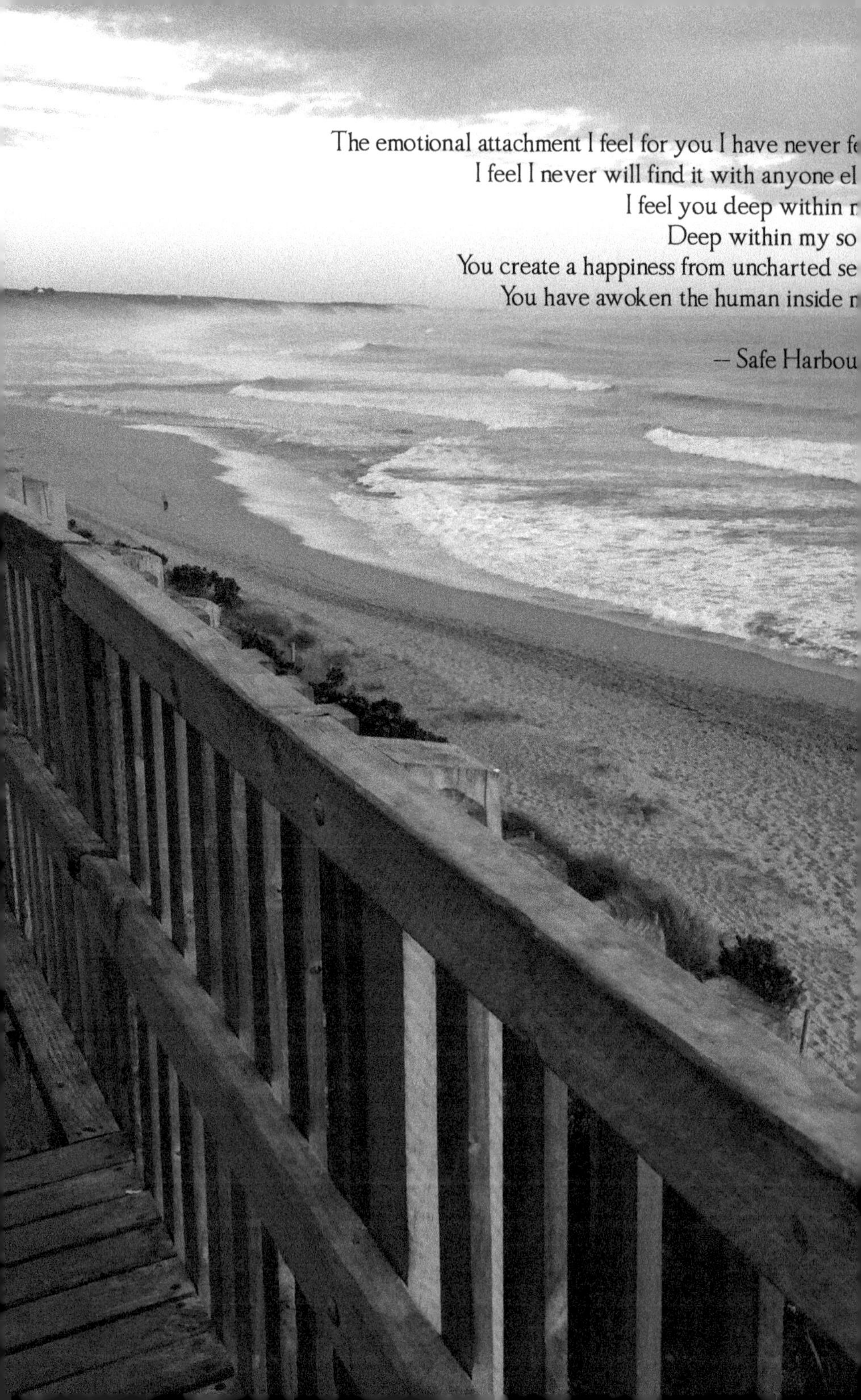

The emotional attachment I feel for you I have never f
I feel I never will find it with anyone el
I feel you deep within m
Deep within my so
You create a happiness from uncharted se
You have awoken the human inside m

– Safe Harbou

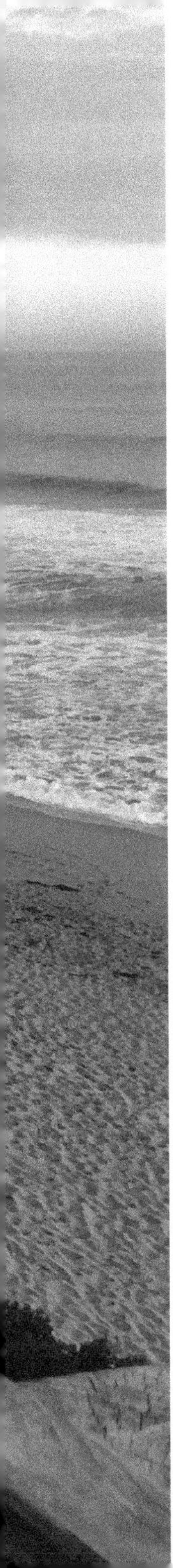

What can it be?
A look that I see
A connection with thee
For when it arrives
What will it be
The feeling of love

-- The love inside me

My mindset challenges itself

It remembers all that it's felt

I welcome the warmth of this light

I am forever grateful for this sight.

-- The writer's relief

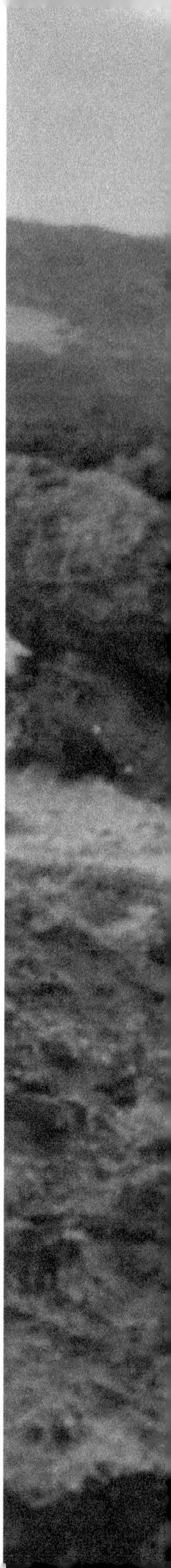

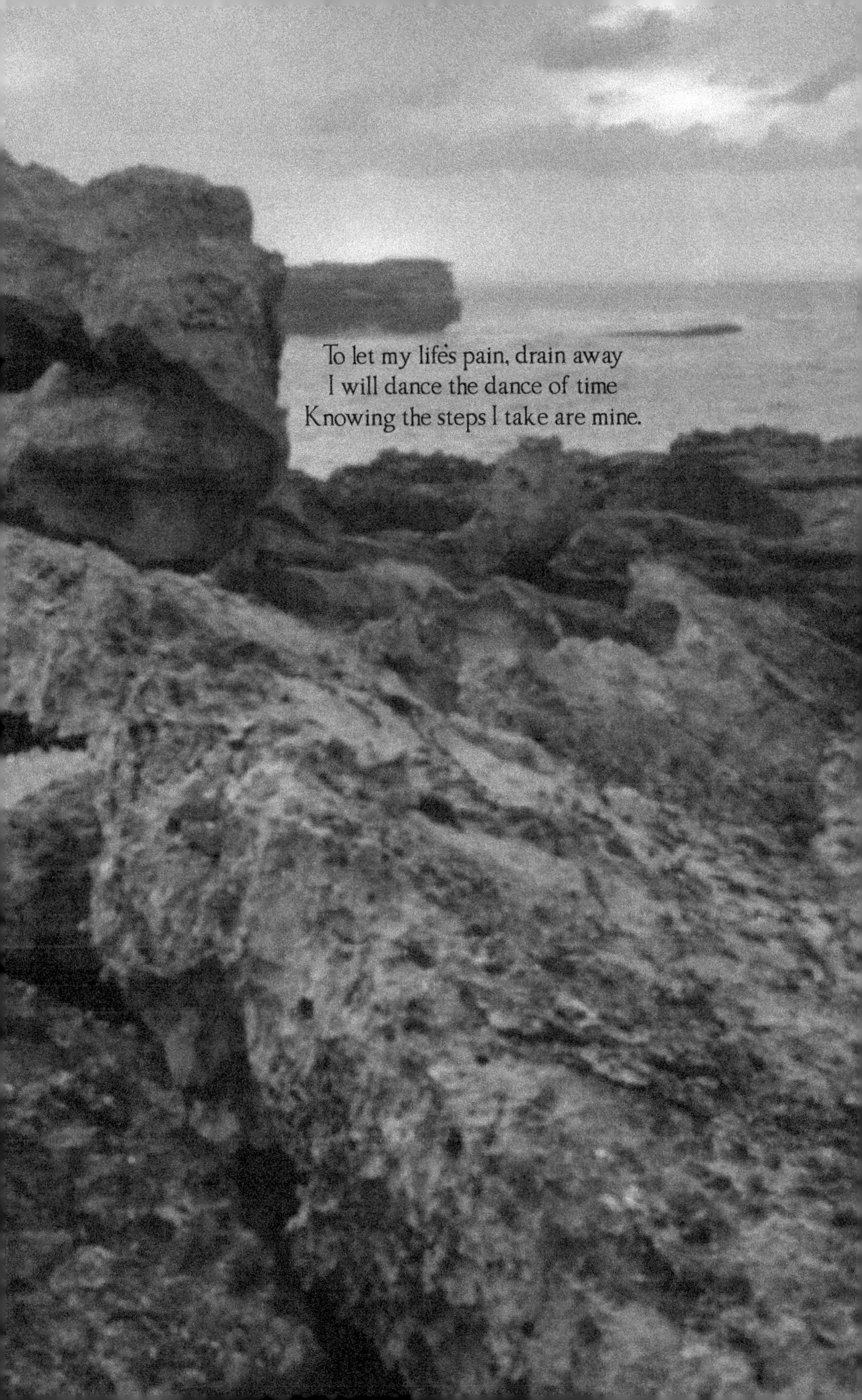

To let my life's pain, drain away
I will dance the dance of time
Knowing the steps I take are mine.

Take my heart and care for it

-- it's ready

CPSIA information can be obtained
at www.ICGtesting.com
Printed in the USA
LVHW071908020521
686270LV00005B/548

9 780648 712749